# Intermediate
# Matters

**JAN BELL**
**ROGER GOWER**

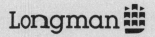

**Longman Group UK Limited,**
*Longman House, Burnt Mill, Harlow,*
*Essex CM20 2JE, England*
*and Associated Companies throughout the world.*

First published 1991

Set in Adobe ITC Garamond Light 10/12pt
and Frutiger Light 8$^1/_2$/10pt

Printed and bound in Great Britain by
BPCC Hazell Books
Aylesbury, Bucks, England
Member of BPCC Ltd.
ISBN 0 582 04667 X

## Authors' Acknowledgements

We would like to thank the following people.
- Sara Humphreys who provided invaluable ideas.
- Marc Beeby and Gillie Cunningham for allowing us to use some of their material.
- Pat Mugglestone and Richard Rossner for their support and advice.
- Those people who piloted and/or reported on the materials: Donald Adamson, Sarah Aitken, Belinda Baldwin, David Barnett, Richard Cook, Olivia Date, Madeleine du Vivier, Kathy Ellis, Alison Goosey, Sherry Johnston, Rob Jones, Joanne Kenworthy, Chris Lloyd, Helen Naylor, Janet Olearski, Paul Radley, Sarah Scott-Malden, Beverly Sedley, Lindy Seton Winton, Brian Tomlinson and Ann Wills.
- Those people who agreed to be interviewed for our recordings: Bonnie Appleyard, Emma Attwood, Marc Beeby, Sue Boardman, David Bowker, Julie Camman, Jenny Craig, Robin Davis, Judi Dench, Ben Duncan, Pam Gadsby, Marie Gower, Mike Gutteridge, Ed Hackett, Sara Humphreys, Bruce Martin, Bruce Milne, Kevin Moll, the children from Saint Thomas More School, Françoise Mouchet, Simon Mould, Nancy Osmond, Norma Perry, Keith Ricketts, Annie Roberts, Sarah Scott-Malden, Sue Sheerin, Dany Silvarolli, Jane Southwell and Liz Watson.
- Our publishers, Kate Goldrick and Gill Negus; our editors Kate Lovell and Joy Marshall; our designer, Sharon Sutcliffe; as well as Lynette Corner (permissions editor), Yolanda Durham (secretary), John Newton (audio producer), Martine Parsons (production manager), Marilyn Rawlings (art editor) and Clare Sleven (cover designer) – all at Longman ELT.
- The staffs of the Bell School, Cambridge and Bell College, Saffron Walden for their support and cooperation.
- Finally, special thanks should go to our Project Manager, Desmond O'Sullivan of ELT Publishing Services, for coordinating every aspect of the project with such professionalism and for his boundless energy and uncomplaining cheerfulness.

# Contents

# Introduction

## Who is *Intermediate Matters* for?

*Intermediate Matters* is a multisyllabus, theme-based course intended for adults at an intermediate level of English. It aims to provide approximately 120 hours of classroom material. It is suitable for students on intensive courses as well as those on courses for a single academic year. It can be used in either a multilingual or a monolingual classroom situation. Students who successfully complete *Intermediate Matters* can continue their studies with *Upper Intermediate Matters*.

The course material has been piloted in schools in Britain and overseas.

## Guiding principles

*Intermediate Matters* aims to distil the best of current classroom practice. It balances many different elements: both inductive and deductive approaches to grammar awareness; accuracy with fluency in speaking and writing; controlled practice with affective personalised activities; and tried-and-tested approaches with new ideas. As a way of integrating the work of each unit, we have used generative, human-interest topics, lively extracts from journalism and literature, and manageable authentic listening texts. From our experience of teaching at this level, such texts are effective in motivating students to speak and write. Systematic attention has also been given to such often neglected areas as vocabulary, writing and pronunciation, and emphasis given to developing learning strategies in order to encourage learner-independence. Overall, *Intermediate Matters* provides sophisticated, motivating material to meet the practical needs of teachers and students alike.

## The intermediate student

At this level students usually have some knowledge of the main grammatical areas of English and a basic, if restricted, vocabulary. Nevertheless, students are frequently unable to use what they know appropriately, accurately and confidently in a real-life communicative situation.

One of the difficulties in teaching an intermediate class (particularly an adult class) is that students often come from a variety of learning backgrounds and have a range of different learning abilities. Some students can communicate quite fluently whereas others are very hesitant. Some are used to listening to natural connected speech; others have only ever listened to scripted texts. A lot of students find accurate writing a major problem.

For some students, many of the language structures will be relatively unfamiliar; other students will seem disillusioned at being taught the same structures over and over again. This latter group may have been struggling for years to break through the learning 'plateau' that is often reached at this level, a lack of progress leading to frustration and poor motivation.

## Components

### 1 Students' Book and Class Cassettes

The Students' Book consists of twenty units of which the first four are *Review* units and the last unit is devoted to revision. Each unit aims to provide between four and a half and six hours classroom work. Pairs of units (with the exception of Units 19 and 20) are linked by a common theme, even though each unit has its own separate topic focus. The *Contents chart* at the beginning of the Students' Book (and repeated in the Teacher's Book) provides a breakdown of the topics, language and skills covered in each unit.

Each unit can be divided roughly into three 'blocks' of which the middle block usually (but not always) provides the language focus. In the first block there is generally a reading or a listening text, and in most cases this alternates from unit to unit. (However, if the main focus of the Students' Book unit is listening, then the main focus of the Workbook unit is reading, and vice versa.) Example (Students' Book: Review Unit 3):

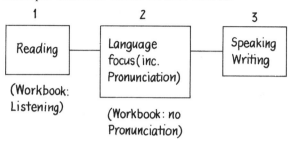

As a rule, each unit includes:
- both *Listening* and *Reading* texts as a basis for either language or skills work.
- one or more *Vocabulary* sections.
- a *Writing* section.
- one or more *Grammar* points.
*Pronunciation* is usually to be found in every second unit.

Each unit (with the exception of Unit 20) has a *Language reference* page which summarises the language covered in the unit. While working on a particular unit students are frequently referred to specific sections in the corresponding *Language reference*.

There is also useful support material at the back of the Students' Book. This consists of a summary of verb forms, an irregular verbs list, a pronunciation chart, a writing reference section, as well as the tapescripts of most of the recordings used in the Students' Book.

The two Class Cassettes contain all the recordings used in the Students' Book.

A split edition of the Students' Book (Students' Book A and Students' Book B) is also available. The split edition does not contain the *Tapescripts* section.

## 2 Workbook and Students' Cassette

The Workbook provides support for the Students' Book. It can be used for homework, for further practice in class, or as material to be worked on in a self-access centre. The Workbook and the Students' Cassette contain extra practice (and sometimes extension) of the main language areas of the Students' Book unit (including pronunciation in every other unit).

There is a *Contents chart* at the front of the Workbook so that teachers and students can quickly locate what they want to practise.

Each Workbook unit, with the exception of Unit 20 which is a revision unit, contains either a listening or a reading text.

The Workbook is available with or without a key to the exercises. A split edition (Workbook A and Workbook B – with *Key*) is also available.

A single Students' Cassette contains all the recorded material needed for the listening and pronunciation exercises in the Workbook. The listening material is mostly authentic and is linked in topic to the corresponding Students' Book units. The Students' Cassette allows students to listen to material in their own time, using their own cassette recorders. This gives slower learners the opportunity to work at their own pace and develop greater confidence.

## 3 Teacher's Book

Each unit of the Teacher's Book opens with a summary of the material covered in the Students' Book and the Workbook. This opening section also shows how the Students' Book unit can be broken down roughly into three 'blocks' of work (each lasting at least one and a half hours). The Teacher's Book then goes on to provide:
- information on the language points of the unit. (Common student errors are indicated by a preceding asterisk.)
- notes on many of the exercises (except where the Students' Book rubrics are self-explanatory).
- indications of where material in the Workbook can be suitably integrated into the course.
- the tapescripts of all the recordings on the Class Cassettes as well as a key to the Students' Book exercises.

Indexes at the back of the Teacher's Book give the teacher easy reference and access to all the language points in both the Students' Book and the Workbook.

# Key features

## 1 Content

Motivating content is a key feature of *Intermediate Matters*. The course contains a wide range of human-interest topics. These texts often provide new angles on familiar areas and encourage students to talk about their own experience and make contrasts with their own culture.

## 2 Grammar

The course focuses on items of language that are systematic and rule-based and that can generate different types of utterance in different contexts. The presentation of these language items is sometimes followed up by activities which require students to work out for themselves the meaning and form of the items. At all times students get the opportunity to practise the language items through a range of semi-controlled and communicative activities.

At the end of each unit (with the exception of Unit 20) there is a *Language reference* section containing an easy-to-follow summary of the main points of the unit.

## 3 Vocabulary

The reading and listening texts are often authentic, which means that they frequently have a vocabulary load which is a little higher than might be expected at this level.

The aim of the vocabulary syllabus is to promote acquisition from the texts, systematic word-building skills and lexical development from the practice exercises, as well as good study habits in the learner development activities.

## 4 Receptive skills

With the receptive skills of listening and reading, attention has been focused on the macro and micro skills involved in the understanding of authentic and adapted-authentic texts.

## 5 Productive skills

With the productive skills of speaking and writing a clear distinction has been made between *practising* language in a controlled way and *using* language more freely. Each unit attempts to provide a balance between accuracy-based and fluency-based work.

## 6 Pronunciation

Practical pronunciation work (in both the Students' Book and the Workbook) focuses attention on intonation in connected speech, word and sentence stress, and segmented sounds, including weak forms. It also places emphasis on finding out how to look up pronunciation and word stress in the dictionary so that students will be able to continue to improve their pronunciation outside the classroom.

## 7 Learner development

While study skills, such as using dictionaries and keeping vocabulary records, are explicitly developed, learner development is implicit throughout the course.

## 8 Revision and recycling

The first four units are referred to as *Review units* because they aim not to 'present' the language to students but to get students to activate what they should already know. To this end students are exposed to accessible authentic reading and/or listening texts selected to stimulate oral and written fluency and encourage the use of the key language areas (e.g. present or past verb forms).

# Methodology

## 1 General principles

### Exposure
Authentic human-interest texts form the core of most of the units. This is based on our belief that interesting topics stimulate personal involvement and motivation and therefore encourage spoken and written use of the language. We also believe that exposure to global, unsimplified language is very important at this level. Activities which go with the reading and listening texts aim to build learners' confidence and develop their strategies for reading and listening outside the classroom.

## Accuracy

An eclectic approach has been taken to the introduction of language points to allow for students' different learning styles. We believe in plenty of revision, with 'old' language constantly being recycled and contrasted with 'new' uses of the language in order to enable learners to make the right choices in communicative situations.

There is a lot of opportunity to practise the target language in a controlled way. However even when the focus is on accuracy, the exercises are frequently personalised and interactive.

Pronunciation work is also often accuracy-focused, (for example with work on sounds and word stress). Writing activities provide extra language practice as well as introducing such formal features as punctuation, spelling, organisation and layout.

## Use

It is important that learners experiment with the language and develop their fluency. Many of the grammar or vocabulary activities are interactive and best done in pairs or groups. In the SPEAKING sections there is specific emphasis on communicative fluency, and many of the activities in the WRITING sections encourage students to be creative.

Communicative use is also important with vocabulary and pronunciation. The topic-based approach to the units encourages students to put the vocabulary studied to immediate active use. Attention has also been paid to the communicative importance of appropriate sentence stress and intonation.

## Learning strategies

Help given in the development of learning strategies forms a fundamental element of the course. Students learn to take responsibilty for monitoring their speaking and writing and develop strategies for coping with authentic texts. Students are also made aware of the importance of vocabulary and are helped with techniques for extending their vocabulary both inside and outside the classroom.

## 2 The role of the teacher

Given the general principles outlined above it is clear that the teacher's role needs to be both flexible and supportive.

### Flexible

If necessary the material in each unit can in many cases be re-ordered, cut and supplemented according to the needs of the students and the time available; and the methodology suggested in the Students' Book (e.g. working in groups) can be adapted to the realities of a particular classroom situation (e.g. if there is too little time for a groupwork activity it might be done as a whole class activity).

One possibility is to have an 'integrated skills' approach: for example, a reading or listening text followed by some vocabulary and/or discussion and then some grammar work.

> Reading/Listening → Vocabulary/Discussion → Grammar

Alternatively it might be preferable to have one lesson based on 'language' (for example, grammar and/or vocabulary and pronunciation) and a separate lesson based on 'skills' (listening and speaking and/or reading and writing).

> Language (Grammar/Vocabulary + Pronunciation)

> THEN

> Skills (Listening + Speaking / Reading + Writing)

Here are some other possible adaptations to a unit:
- Focus on the key language point of the unit in a reading text and then go straight into the LANGUAGE POINT section without necessarily completing all the post-reading activities.
- Use the last of the three blocks of the unit first rather than last. If they are fluency activities, such as discussion, they could well help to highlight the language problems to be focused on in the accuracy work.

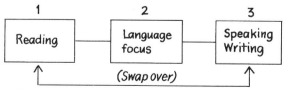

- Vary when the *Language reference* page is referred to according to the specific needs of the class.

– Weave Workbook practice into the sequence in order to give more controlled practice in particular language areas.
– Re-allocate some of the more free-standing sections of the Students' Book (e.g. VOCABULARY skills work, WRITING) to completely different stages of a lesson.

### Supportive

Apart from the usual support and encouragement a teacher gives, there should be systematic help with using dictionaries and grammar books, keeping vocabulary records, revising what students have learned, etc.

## 3 Vocabulary

Vocabulary is given a high priority in the course and is approached in a number of different ways.
– Students are taught and encouraged to guess and deduce the meaning of new words from the context in listening and reading texts.
– Guidance is given on how to make best use of dictionaries. For this reason, it is advisable to help your students assess and choose an appropriate monolingual dictionary. The *Longman Active Study Dictionary* is at an appropriate level and includes exercises to help teachers supplement whatever dictionary work is done in class. The *Longman Dictionary of Contemporary English* is a little more detailed and has a Workbook to go with it (see *Bibliography*). If students also wish to use a bilingual dictionary, encourage them to use a good, fairly comprehensive bilingual dictionary rather than just a small pocket edition.
– Words are studied through word fields, prefixes and suffixes, synonyms and antonyms. Attention is also given to connotation, collocation and phrasal verbs.
– Students are shown ways of approaching their own vocabulary learning (e.g. through keeping organised vocabulary records in vocabulary notebooks).
– Attention is paid to the pronunciation (and word stress) of new words, spelling and the link between sound and spelling.

It is worth remembering that while students will make personal decisions about the words they want to learn and remember, the teacher will need to make some judgement as to which words in a text it would be most useful for them to practise.

Also, the teacher should create opportunites in the classroom for recycling and revising vocabulary. This might be done regularly at the beginning of each lesson.

Try to encourage students to read and listen to as much authentic English as possible (see section 5 below) so that they will acquire vocabulary outside as well as inside the classroom.

## 4 Grammar and functions

In *Intermediate Matters* higher priority has been given to grammatical than to functional labels and descriptions, except where the functions are grammatically generative (e.g. *obligation*). However, some of the less generative functions, such as *agreeing/disagreeing*, are introduced and practised in both the SPEAKING and WRITING sections.

Each unit (with the exception of Unit 20) has a structural or functional area as the main language focus. Learners are encouraged to be clear about how the language item is used and what it means (sometimes referred to as the 'concept' in the Teacher's Book).

In the LANGUAGE POINTS a variety of ways of introducing the language have been included, both inductive and deductive, as appropriate. Students either try to analyse the language and work out a 'rule' (of form or use) from examples or are given explicit descriptions. They are frequently referred to the *Language reference* section at the end of each unit for support, since at this level it may not be advisable to spend too much time on 'analysis' but instead move quickly from example to practice. This eclectic approach is intended to appeal to students with different learning styles.

A number of forms are presented by contrasting one with another (e.g. *will* and *going to* in Unit 5) – particularly those it can be assumed students have already been taught separately on previous occasions. There is also frequent re-cycling of areas of language in subsequent units, further practice in the Workbook and revision in Unit 20.

In general, at this level there is a need for lots of opportunities for practice, in both controlled and freer communicative situations, and both of these kinds of practice have been provided for. The focus in the Students' Book is more on personalised oral activities, but these are supplemented by written exercises in the Workbook, which can also be used in class as back-up.

## 5 Reading

Most of the texts are authentic or adapted-authentic, and will be above the productive level of the students. The main aim is to expose students to as much language as possible and to develop confidence in reading by systematically giving practice in the main sub-skills (e.g. reading for gist).

The texts also help students to acquire new language from a variety of natural contexts as well as to consolidate language which they already know. Some texts can also be used as models for the students' own writing.

As with the listening texts, students are usually asked to do tasks *before* they read a text. This is done in order to: motivate them to read; give a realistic purpose for their reading; and focus their attention on specific areas of the text (either for gist or detailed reading). In many cases these activities also generate some of the vocabulary which is likely to come up in the text. To help determine the level of detail at which students should work on the text the teacher might also like to set a specific time limit for the actual reading stage.

As well as the skills of prediction, and reading for gist and for detail, attention has also been paid in the course to understanding what is said '*between* the lines' (i.e. inference) and the style in which a text is written.

It is a good idea to try and encourage students to read (and listen to) English for pleasure (e.g. if possible, read magazines and listen to the radio). Wall displays of authentic reading material can help to stimulate interest, as can class libraries of readers and magazines.

## 6 Listening

Spoken texts include unscripted interviews and discussions which highlight a range of features of natural connected speech. These recordings have been made outside the studio with a variety of different people. There are also songs and excerpts from radio programmes. In all cases recordings have been carefully chosen to be both interesting and accessible.

As with reading, the emphasis is on teaching students *how* to listen, by directing their attention exclusively to particular elements of a text. The aim is not to test the students (i.e. get them to listen and then check comprehension). To this end the teacher needs to direct students away from trying to understand every word and instead encourage them to concentrate specifically on

what is demanded in the exercises accompanying the text.

Other tips for giving support during the listening activities:

– Teach some of the difficult words or do prediction work on the content of a text beforehand.
– Use the pause button to stop the tape from time to time for reflection/discussion on what is being said, or to focus on features of connected speech such as linkage, intonation, hesitation devices, repetition, etc.
– Allow students to follow the tapescript while they listen (particularly during the second or third time, or if they are finding the text especially difficult). (Note that the *Tapescripts* are not included in the split edition of the Students' Book.)
– Allow students to give their personal response to what they hear (both to the content and the level of difficulty).

## 7 Speaking

When setting up an activity or introducing a text it is often a good idea to elicit ideas, vocabulary, etc. from the students or let students brainstorm ideas/language in pairs or groups.

### Controlled practice

Many of the oral PRACTICE activities are personalised and open-ended, with students encouraged to talk about their own lives and interests.

As the focus in controlled activities is on *accuracy*, it is important that errors are picked up and corrected either by the teacher or by other students. One technique is for the teacher to write down errors as they occur in the activity and get students to correct them in groups. Another is to turn correction into a communicative activity or a game. See for example, 'Auction', 'Snakes and ladders', 'Correcting homework' and 'Mistakes dictation' in *Grammar Games* (see *Bibliography*).

The teacher may like to supplement controlled practice done in this course with practice activities from books such as *Grammar Games* and *Grammar Practice Activities* (see *Bibliography*).

### Speaking

In the SPEAKING sections the emphasis is mainly on *fluency* and activating vocabulary, and the teacher's role is to monitor the students' English and give some feedback on it (e.g. by suggesting improvements, giving ideas, correcting mistakes, etc.). Sometimes the teacher might want to participate in an activity as an 'equal' rather than as a teacher who controls and checks. Some of the SPEAKING activities need careful setting up and preparation. In some monolingual classes the teacher might want to explain the purpose of the activity and give instructions in the students' mother tongue.

Many SPEAKING activities (except perhaps the discussions) can be structured in such a way that there is rehearsal in 'closed groups' (with other students or the teacher giving ideas for improvement) followed by performance (either to other groups / the whole class or recorded on to audio/video tape).

Freer communication activities in this book can be supplemented by further activities from books such as *Keep Talking* and *Discussions that Work* (see *Bibliography*) depending on the needs and expectations of students.

## 8 Writing

### Controlled

In general, written language demands greater planning and more accuracy than spoken language. Because of this, many of the WRITING activities are relatively controlled and work from models or are cued, and frequently they combine with consolidation tasks. For example, an introduction to letter-writing might be linked to:
– reinforcement of areas of language that have been learned and practised orally.
– practice of linguistic features commonly found in writing.
– an introduction to more functional language.
In the Review units at the beginning of the course there is a overview of features such as punctuation, spelling and linking expressions. Students are then encouraged to monitor all the written work they do with reference to these features. They are also advised to use the sections on linkers and punctuation on page 150 in the Students' Book as well as the notes on spelling strategies in Review Unit 4.

### Creative

Other writing activities are creative and personal, using such stimuli as discussion and story-telling to get students to focus on w*hat* they are saying rather than *how* they are saying it. They allow the students to express themselves freely, while at the same time encouraging them to use actively the vocabulary which has come up in the unit.

On some occasions it is recommended that students do a draft of the writing task, get other students to cooperate and suggest improvements (or check their own writing for specific mistakes), and then finally redraft it. The teacher will probably need to tell students that they are going to treat their writing in this way and explain the purpose of this approach. (Students learn more effectively by concentrating on the 'process' of writing than by rushing too quickly into a finished 'product'. Students benefit more from correcting their own or each others' errors during the process stages than from when the finished product is corrected or marked by the teacher.)

Other tips:
– Many students are often 'blocked' by not knowing what to write. So when setting up a writing task, brainstorm ideas about content (and language) from the class and start the activity off on the board (eliciting ideas from the students).
– Tell students at the start of the activity whether they are expected to be accurate or fluent.
– Try as far as possible to get students to improve their own / each other's written work (a 'marking' scheme is suggested in Review Unit 4).
– Sometimes tell students that in a particular exercise only one aspect of their work is to be evaluated (e.g. layout, punctuation, etc.) and mark it or indicate errors accordingly. This helps learners improve one problem area at a time and prevents them from getting discouraged.
– When students have written a 'product' which they are satisfied with, get them to display it on the wall for other students to read.
– If working in Britain, get students to write real communications (e.g. a letter of enquiry to a travel agent) and try to get a response.

## 9 Pronunciation

The pronunciation syllabus focuses on areas of difficulty: e.g. discrimination between particular consonants and vowel sounds (including diphthongs), vowel reduction (i.e. weak forms), word stress, sentence stress, sound linking and the intonation of requests.

While for the most part pronunciation exercises can be found every second unit, it is suggested that

on-going attention is given to pronunciation rather than devoting specific lessons to this area of the language. For example:
- When a new word is introduced, practise its sounds and word stress (using dictionaries for assistance on some occasions).
- When setting up semi-controlled pairwork (e.g. cued dialogues) anticipate areas of pronunciation difficulty and practise them.
- In a roleplay or when listening to a recording, point out the communicative effect of the intonation (e.g. *'Does he/she sound rude? Bored? Why?'*).
- Encourage students to identify their pronunciation problems and work on them by themselves, if possible using a language laboratory or their own personal cassette recorders. This is particularly important with multilingual groups. The teacher might find it useful to refer to information in *Better English Pronunciation, Sounds English, Ship or Sheep?, Teaching English Pronunciation*, or *Learner English* (see *Bibliography*).

Other tips:
- Decide on a policy for marking stress on the board (e.g. a ' as in dictionaries, a box or a circle?) and try to be consistent.
- Decide on the role of the phonemic alphabet (on page 149 of the Students' Book). Will it be used only as a reference during dictionary work? Will it be used as a prompt for pronunciation correction? Should there be systematic training in the sounds followed by a linking of the sounds to the symbols? etc.
- Link sound and spelling as far as possible in English. (There are exercises in the Workbook on pages 27, 41, and 69 and also in the *Spelling* section in *Sounds English* – see *Bibliography*.)

Teachers might like to supplement classroom practice with exercises from books such as *Ship or Sheep?, Sounds English* and *Speaking Clearly* (see *Bibliography*).

# Acknowledgement

We are grateful to Robert Hill for his suggestions and comments on the Lan*guage* section in each unit.

# Abbreviations

| | |
|---|---|
| T | Teacher |
| SS | Students |
| SB | Students' Book |
| WB | Workbook |
| TB | Teacher's Book |
| GW | groupwork |
| PW | pairwork |
| OHT | overhead transparency |

# Contents chart (Students' Book)

| Unit | Topics | Grammar/functions | Vocabulary |
|---|---|---|---|
| **1** | Leisure activities | Likes and dislikes<br>Definite article<br>*So do I./ Neither do I. Do you? I don't.*<br>Question forms with Present Simple<br>Less direct questions<br>Short form answers | Leisure activities<br>Adjectives and verbs of likes and dislikes |
| **2** | Clothes and appearance | Present Simple with frequency adverbs/phrases<br>Present Continuous | Clothes |
| **3** | Adventures abroad | Past Simple and Continuous<br>*Used to*<br>Time prepositions<br>Suggestions, opinions, agreeing/disagreeing | Nationality words |
| **4** | Living in Britain | Present Perfect (past experience, indefinite time)<br>Time expressions<br>Question tags | Deducing meaning |
| **5** | Weather | Predictions and decisions (*will* and *going to*)<br>Verbs and prepositions | Weather |
| **6** | The environment | Defining relative clauses<br>Clauses of purpose | Adjectives ending in *-ed* and *-ing*<br>Word building with suffixes |
| **7** | People and relationships | Asking for descriptions<br>Adjective word order<br>Possessive *-s*<br>Adverbs of manner and degree | Describing personality and appearance |
| **8** | Homes | Prepositions of place<br>Comparisons<br>Adverbs of degree | Making opposites |
| **9** | Signs and predictions | Open conditionals: promises, threats, warnings<br>Modal auxiliaries: levels of certainty<br>*Unless* | Illness<br>Antonyms and synonyms |
| **10** | Houses of the future | Time conjunctions with the present<br>*If* or *when?*<br>Future Passive<br>Future arrangements | Phrasal verbs with *up* and *down* |
| **11** | Hotels and restaurants | Requests<br>Agreeing and offering<br>Refusing, making excuses | Hotels<br>Changing verbs into nouns<br>Food |
| **12** | Money | Second conditional<br>*Wish* + past tense | Money<br>Theft |
| **13** | Eccentric people | *Since/for*<br>Present Perfect (unfinished past) | Colloquial English: slang; idiomatic expressions |
| **14** | Unusual hobbies | Obligation, prohibition, permission | Leisure<br>Words often confused |
| **15** | Food and health | Quantity | Deducing words in context<br>Phrasal verbs |
| **16** | Unusual animals | Reported speech | Animals<br>Idiomatic expressions (animals) |
| **17** | Phobias | *-ing* or *to?* | Fear<br>Changing adjectives into verbs |
| **18** | The unexpected | Past Perfect Simple and Continuous | *Make* or *do?* |
| **19** | Prejudice | The passive | Collocation |
| **20** | Revision | Integrated skills and language revision | |

| Pronunciation | Writing |
| --- | --- |
| Word stress<br>Intonation in questions<br>Weak form of *do* in questions | Personal information |
| Present Simple endings<br>Linking in connected speech | Punctuation |
| Past Simple endings<br>Weak forms of *was/were* in<br>  Past Continuous<br>*Used to* | Linking expressions<br>Narrative (from sounds) |
| Intonation in question tags<br>Contracted forms of Present<br>  Perfect | Spelling |
| Contracted form of *will*<br>Weak form of *to* in *going to* | Telephone dialogue |
| Syllable stress: schwa (/ə/) | Semi-formal letter<br>Clauses of reason and result |
| – | Personal letter |
| Word stress | Linking expressions<br>Description of a place |
| – | Connecting sentences to make<br>  a narrative |
| Vowels | Styles of writing |
| Intonation of requests | Notes and messages |
| – | Letter of advice |
| Sentence stress | Summary |
| *Have to, must* | Opening and closing a letter<br>Letter of application |
| Consonants (voiced/unvoiced) | Report |
| – | Descriptive writing (poem) |
| Diphthongs | Linking words and expressions |
| – | Comparing narrative styles |
| Contrastive stress | Story |

---

### Learning strategies

The development of *Learning strategies* is integral to all units. The following units include explicit *Learning strategies* activities: Review Unit 2 (Guessing meaning from grammatical context); Review Unit 3 (Using a monolingual dictionary; Guessing meaning; Keeping vocabulary records); Review Unit 4 (Keeping a grammar book; Approaches to language learning; Learner diaries).

---

### Reading, Listening, Speaking

Each unit has either a *Reading* or a *Listening* skills focus (*Reading/Listening* for gist, detail and interpretation). Each unit also has at least one communicative *Speaking* activity (e.g. discussion, roleplay).

# Contents chart (Workbook)

| Reading | Listening | Writing | Pronunciation |
| --- | --- | --- | --- |
| Magazine article | – | Daily routine | – |
| – | – | Punctuation; dictation | – |
| Newspaper article; vocabulary in context | – | – | – |
| – | Two people describing learning a language | Dictation | – |
| Short story extract | – | – | Different words, same pronunciation |
| – | Children talking about the environment | Semi-formal / personal writing; dictation | – |
| Novel extract | – | – | Sound and spelling |
| – | Interview with an estate agent | Linking expressions | – |
| Magazine article | – | – | Word stress |
| – | Two people talking about the future | Spelling | – |
| – | Sketches of different people at work | Dialogue | Short and long vowels; sound and spelling |
| Magazine article | – | Dictation | Vowel sounds |
| – | Three people talking about their dreams | Summary writing | – |
| Jigsaw text | – | Punctuation and layout; abbreviations | Weak forms |
| – | Ed talking about what he eats | Advertisement | – |
| Magazine article | – | Direct speech | Problem consonants |
| – | Four people talking about their fears | Story | – |
| Magazine extracts | – | – | Diphthongs |
| – | Nancy on her experience of sexism | Similar spellings | Contrastive stress; silent letters |
| – | – | Linking expressions; dictation | Sounds |

# My favourite things

## Students' Book

**General theme:** people.
**Unit topic:** leisure activities.

**SPEAKING 1:** finding out about people's interests.
**READING:** an article about comedian Lenny Henry's likes and dislikes.
**VOCABULARY:** adjectives and verbs of likes and dislikes.

**GRAMMAR REVIEW 1:** verbs followed by -ing; similarities (*So do I. / Neither do I. / I do, too.*) and differences (*Do you? I don't.*).
**PRONUNCIATION:** intonation of questions; weak form of *do*.
**GRAMMAR REVIEW 2:** question forms; short answers.

**LISTENING:** interview with actress, Judi Dench.
**GRAMMAR REVIEW 3:** the definite article; direct and less direct questions.
**SPEAKING 2:** interviewing someone about their life and interests.
**WRITING:** writing up personal information.

## Workbook

**READING:** magazine article about actress Jenny Agutter's typical Sunday; verbs followed by -ing; question forms; short answers.
**VOCABULARY:** strong adjectives (e.g. *filthy*); housework; everyday expressions.
**GRAMMAR:** less direct questions; the definite article; *So do I. / Neither do I.*
**WRITING:** paragraph about a typical Sunday.

## Language

The language focus in this unit is on question forms in the present (direct and less direct); short answers; verbs (of likes and dislikes) followed by -ing; similarities and differences (*So do I. / Neither do I.; Do you? I don't.*); and the definite article (use and omission of *the* for general and specific things). It is assumed that, at this level, SS will 'know' all or most of these items. However, they may not be using them accurately. Notice that this unit looks at the pronunciation of these areas as well as the grammar.

The principle objective of the unit is to get SS to find out each others' names and more information about one another. The focus for the SS is therefore on personalised communication activities, through which it is hoped that they will be encouraged to use the target language naturally.

It is important at the beginning of a new course that intermediate SS do not feel they are covering old ground yet again. That is why there is a range of activities in the unit which have a communicative aim – the focus being on *using* language, rather than analysing it. However, the language which should come out of these activities is fairly predictable (listed above) and you will be able to see how much remedial work (in the GRAMMAR REVIEW sections) he or she needs to do.

If SS are making mistakes, make a note of them and tell SS what they are after the activity. Alternatively, get SS to use your notes to correct their own mistakes (see the *Introduction* for ways of doing this).

If SS use language in a less controlled situation and have their attention drawn to their errors or gaps they should then realise what areas they need to do more work on. As a result they will probably be much more receptive to a quick re-presentation of the particular language point (in the GRAMMAR REVIEW sections).

There are extra exercises in the WB on all areas covered in the unit, and these exercises can be used to supplement those in the SB.

## Common problems

### Question forms in the present

**1**   In many languages questions are asked by using the affirmative form with a different intonation, and SS may transfer this into English. A typical mistake would be: *You like tennis?*

**2**   Since there is no *do/does* equivalent in other languages it is not surprising that so many SS are confused about what it means and generally avoid using it.

**3**   Many SS try to keep the *-s* in the third person, (*Does she lives here?*). There is also the danger of overgeneralising *do* and *does* and using it in front of other auxiliaries (*Do you can swim?*).

### Less direct questions

The main problem here is the change of word order (see the *Language reference*). A typical mistake here would be: *Could you tell me where is the bank?* SS also need a lot of help with the appropriate use of less direct questions.

### Short answers

If SS reply *'Yes'* or *'No'* without the auxiliary (*I do / I don't*) the reply can sometimes sound abrupt. SS also have problems using the correct auxiliary (including *do* or *does*). A common error is: *'Do you like riding horses?'* *'Yes I like.'*

### The definite article

A problem with many SS at intermediate and other levels, even those whose system is similar to the English one (e.g. Dutch). In this unit the focus is on the omission of the definite article when talking about things in general and for most countries and languages, and its contrast when talking about specific things. Mistakes occur because:
– many students don't have the definite article in their own language (e.g. Russian or Japanese) and simply leave it out (*Give me pen.*).
– other students (e.g. Italian, Greek) use it in their own language where English doesn't, e.g. for general things (*The tea is not good for you.*).

### So do I. / Neither have I.

SS tend to avoid this construction in favour of *'I do, too.'* or *'Me too.'* When they do use it, common mistakes are:
– the word order (*'So I do.'*).
– failure to use the auxiliary or *do/does* (*'I hate ironing.'* *'So hate I.'*).
– forgetting to stress the contrasting word (*'So do I.'*).

### Do you? I don't.

Students will be familiar with expressions like *'Really?'* to express surprise but probably not with the reply questions common in English, which involve an auxiliary and a personal pronoun. The problems will be with selecting the appropriate auxiliary, and with the intonation (see the *Language reference*). Give lots of practice in this, encouraging SS to exaggerate their intonation.

# SPEAKING 1

## Things people like

Provides an opportunity for SS and T to get to know each other's names and something about each other. You will probably have other 'getting-to-know-you' activities which would work equally well here. However, this activity, as well as giving some idea of SS' level of fluency and vocabulary, is intended to get SS to use particular problem language areas which are followed up later in the GRAMMAR REVIEW sections.

● **Exercise 1**   A quick whole class warm-up to see how much vocabulary SS can generate, and to help them with the next activity. Note that the *hobbies* category could apply to several of the activities in the photographs. Useful revision of common lexical areas. Make sure that SS give the general word first (e.g. *sport*) and then the specific one (e.g. *horse-riding*). Could be done as PW.

● **Exercise 2**   A personalised activity: SS have to write down their own likes and dislikes. An example on the blackboard (based on your own likes and dislikes?) might help to make the activity clearer. Be prepared to help with vocabulary.

● **Exercise 3**   SS need to know exactly what they are doing here, so 'model' it on the board or use one of the tables the SS have produced as an example. With a very large class it might be better to do the mingling activity in largish groups rather than as a complete class. During this activity you should find out a lot about the SS as well as about their language level. Most of the target language will probably come up (verbs of likes and dislikes + *-ing*, question forms, short answers, the article, agreeing, showing differences, etc.) and it will be apparent whether students are using the language accurately or perhaps avoiding it completely.

Resist the temptation to correct on the spot as the main aim here is communication.

● **Exercise 4** *Both ... and* and *Neither ... nor* can be introduced informally here. Encourage SS to memorise and use names in the feedback. If you are going on to the READING section next it is probably better to save comments on SS' language until later. You might prefer to go directly from the SPEAKING section to specific exercises in the GRAMMAR REVIEW section which SS are having problems with. Obviously, you may not need to do revision on all the areas.

# READING

Use the photo to build up an idea of what Lenny Henry might be like before SS read the text. Possibly extend this into a discussion on what kind of comedians SS like and how humour differs in different countries. An opportunity to introduce an expression that comes up in the text (*stand-up comedy*) as well as other descriptions of humour.

● **Exercises 1 and 2** SS read the text quickly in order to pick out Lenny Henry's likes from the first three paragraphs, and his dislikes from the last two paragraphs. (You may need to explain some of the new vocabulary: *soap opera, CDs, baggy suits, racist*). Try to discourage SS from asking too many questions about vocabulary of likes and dislikes – this is the focus of the next activity. Encourage SS to focus on finding information about Lenny Henry and to make *brief* notes, as in the examples. SS could then compare their notes (PW). In the feedback you might like to ask SS to talk about what they found out, and compare it to what they found out about people in the class.

● **Exercise 3** An alternative to doing this in pairs would simply be a quick informal class discussion of some or all of the points.

# VOCABULARY

## Likes and dislikes: adjectives

● **Exercise 1** A good opportunity to introduce SS to looking up words in a monolingual dictionary such as *Longman Active Study Dictionary*, or *Longman Dictionary of Contemporary English* (see *Bibliography*).

● **Exercise 2** Make clear to SS what a syllable is by 'modelling' *fan•tas•tic* for them. However, there is more work on this in Unit 8. Discuss which method of marking stress you intend to use in class – we have used the convention of putting Æ before a syllable here because it is the one used in many dictionaries, but many Ts find other methods clearer for boardwork, such as a circle or a square above the stressed vowel, or underlining the stressed syllable. If you do use a different convention to the one in the dictionary, however, it is important to show SS how stress is marked in the dictionary you are recommending. Point out or 'elicit' the tendency in English to put the stress on the first syllable in adjectives.

Possibly a good opportunity to introduce the 'strong' adjectives from the WB, or set them as a homework task.

● **Exercises 3 and 4** Gives practice in using adjectives and could either be done individually or as PW, followed by quick reporting back.

## Likes and dislikes: verbs

Make sure SS realise that some of the verbs in the box are much stronger/weaker than others, and cannot be used interchangeably.

# GRAMMAR REVIEW 1

## Verbs + -ing

In this section you may want to introduce SS to the *Language reference* and suggest how it might be used. Remind them that the grammar in this unit is revision, and accuracy should be aimed at.

Elicit or draw SS's attention to the form of the verb after *love* and *doesn't mind*. (Other examples in the text are: *I like **reading** comics.* and *I just adore **listening** to music.*) You could ask SS to try and remember what other people in the class like and dislike doing. Tell SS that the infinitive can also be used after some of these verbs, but that *-ing* is more common. (This comes up again in Unit 17.)

## Similarities and differences

● **Exercise 1**  Point out the weak form of *do/can* in *So do/can I.*, etc. and the linking of words which is common in connected speech, when two vowels together produce an intrusive /w/ sound (e.g. *So do I.*). Get SS to practise this.

Model the intonation for *Do you?* and the contrastive stress in *I don't.* or *So do I.* If you think it is necessary, a short, snappy drill could be done around the class by giving one student a verbal cue (e.g. *going to the cinema*) to generate a stimulus (e.g. *I like/hate going to the cinema.*) for another student to respond to (*So/Neither do I. / Do you? I don't.*). Make it clear that the 'reply question' (*Do you?*) is optional. There is another exercise on this in the WB.

● **Exercise 2**  You may want to encourage SS to think of their own examples too. Monitor pronunciation and intonation as well as grammatical accuracy.

## PRONUNCIATION

● **Exercise 1**  SS need to recognise polite and not so polite intonation patterns, even if they are unable to produce them. Point out the high pitch level for more polite questions and the flatter monotonous tone for not so polite questions. Exaggerate an example in order to get the message across.

● **Exercise 2**  Possibly an opportunity to introduce SS to the *schwa* sound (/ə/) and indicate it on a phonemic chart (see the phonemic chart on SB page 149) or on the board. You might like to point out that in rapid speech *Do you* can also sound like /dʒə/.

## GRAMMAR REVIEW 2

## Question forms and short answers

● **Exercise 1**  Possibly do a couple of examples together before PW. This will enable you to focus on accuracy of question forms and production of short answers as well as the pronunciation and intonation practised in the previous exercise. SS might want to look back at the Lenny Henry text before trying to do this activity.

This could be expanded into a dialogue based on SS' own likes/dislikes, or on personalities that SS know.

## LISTENING

## Before listening

● **Exercises 1 and 2**  Build up interest in Judi Dench by using the pictures for prediction (e.g. *'What do you think her job is? What kind of acting does she do? Who do you think the man in the picture is?'*) and asking SS if they have seen any of her films, TV programmes or theatre productions. Explain that she is not only a well-known Shakespearean actress (see the second photograph of her in *Macbeth* on SB page 8) but has also appeared in many films (see the third photograph of her in *A Room With A View*) and also TV dramas and situational comedies (see the first photograph of her with her husband, Michael Williams, in *A Fine Romance*). For the purposes of the recordings it is important to tell SS that Judi also has a daughter, who is called Finty (or Fint).

Students could work on their questions in pairs. As well as leading to the *Listening* this also gives additional practice in question forms.

## Listening

The recording is authentic, and the speed and naturalness may cause some SS to panic at first if they are only used to listening to simplified language. However, the recording is divided into two parts to make it easier, and the first part will not be too much of a problem for most SS. If it is, it might be worth giving them the second part to work on at their own speed in a language laboratory or on their own personal cassette.

● **Exercise 1**   Notice that the interviewer uses both direct and less direct questions. Possibly highlight the vocabulary of housework (e.g. *ironing*).

● **Exercise 2**   Go over the vocabulary before they listen, checking SS understand and can pronounce the words. Notice Judi uses adjectives such as *great, lovely,* and *wonderful,* as well as verbs + *-ing* (*Michael loves gardening* …). Possibly explain *Hamlet, chamber music* and *veg.*

# GRAMMAR REVIEW 3

## The definite article (*the*)

● **Exercises 1 and 2**   Discuss with SS, pointing out the basic very general 'concept', and the use or omission of the definite article. Do the extra exercise from the WB, either in class or for homework. Possibly also do some extra revision on:
– the difference between the indefinite article, *a/an* (when things are mentioned for the first time) and the definite article (when things have already been referred to).
– other uses of the definite article, such as for some public places (*the cinema, the bank, the hospital*) compared to prepositional phrases such as *in bed, in hospital, at work, at school.*

## Direct and less direct questions

Less direct questions may be new for SS and may need some presentation, perhaps followed up by a quick oral drill to focus on form (transforming direct questions to less direct ones?).

● **Exercise 2**   Intended as controlled practice, which focuses both on form and use.

# SPEAKING 2

## Asking and answering questions

This section aims to give practice in the language points focused on in this unit (grammar, pronunciation and vocabulary); to serve as an opportunity for SS to get to know another (or more than one) person in the class who they haven't yet spoken to; and to provide input to the writing which follows. (You could take part in this activity yourself.) If you are in Britain or have access to native speakers, SS could interview a native speaker instead or as well as other SS. In this, possibly more formal situation, less direct forms would come up more naturally.

# WRITING

## Personal information

A 'process writing' activity (see the *Introduction*), the principle objective being to produce information about somebody in the class, or a native speaker. If possible put the profiles on a classroom wall for other SS to read, together with polaroid snaps of the SS after they have been identified.

The activity and the piece of writing will also serve as a very useful diagnostic instrument for the T. Instead of correcting SS' work you could underline the error and put a symbol in the margin (e.g. *p* for punctuation, *gr* for grammar) – perhaps explaining the rationale behind it to your SS. SS could then correct their own or each other's work. In Review Unit 4 there are suggestions for ways in which Ts can get SS to correct their own writing.

# Tapescripts

## RECORDING 1

a) 'How old are you?'
b) 'Are you married?'
c) 'Have you got any children?'
d) 'Why do you listen to classical music?'
e) 'Where do you work?'
f) 'Can I ask you some questions?'

## RECORDING 2

a) 'Do you like travelling to other countries?'
   'Yes, I do. I go abroad at least twice a year.'
b) 'What do we want to drink?'
   'Let's have a bottle of wine, shall we?'
c) 'Do you ever play tennis?'
   'Yes, I do, but only in the summer.'
d) 'Where do they live?'
   'In Brazil. They really love it there.'

## RECORDING 3

INTERVIEWER: I wonder if you'd mind answering one or two more personal questions. You have a husband who is a well-known actor and you also have a teenage daughter. How do you manage to balance your work life with your home life?

JUDI DENCH: With difficulty! This is, this is the shortest answer you're going to get! It's very, very difficult, especially that we have two houses – luckily that we have two houses – but, still, trying to do the shopping and the laundry and the washing and the ironing, and think about what I need for the weekend, and think about petrol for the car, and think about somebody coming back into the house, you know, all those things, and Michael, of course, and Finty – I mean, they're – I couldn't do it without them 'cause they're just wonderful helps.

I: Have you got any pets?

J: Oh yes, we have three cats, one which won't come back to London – it stays in the country – and two which commute with us, and a dog and a rabbit and two donkeys. (Two donkeys?) They don't come back to London with us, either!

## RECORDING 4

I: I wonder if you would mind telling me some of the things you like doing in your spare time? I mean, for example, sports, hobbies, holidays …

J: Well, yes. I, I trained as a designer, a theatre designer, so I've never given up drawing, and I, I do draw and paint still quite a lot, 'specially on holiday. And we all have a go, 'cause Michael's wonderfully good at it, but he won't say he is, but he is – and Finty's very, very good at it indeed, and she draws all the time, so we do a lot of drawing and painting, and I like cooking, when I have the time to do it, though I don't like doing it under pressure.

I: What kind of things do you like cooking?

J: Well, Michael's a meat and two veg man, so he gets meat and two veg a lot, and that really. Bread and butter pudding – he loves bread and butter pudding, so we do that a lot, 'cause I have a secret recipe – and what else do I do? Michael loves gardening, he's very good at all that, and I've also got a passion for dolls' houses – I have a doll's house which takes up a great deal of my time. I, I love all that, but it's got to be absolutely perfect.

I: Do you like travelling abroad much?

J: Yes, I love it. We love it. (Where, in particular?) I was in Yugoslavia last year, with *Hamlet*, so the whole family – we all went – we had the most wonderful time with the company. We had a great, great time, swimming – we all swim like mad – and that was very good, that was lovely. So we might get back to Yugoslavia in August, I hope we will. We always take August off, 'cause it's Fint's holidays.

I: What, what kind of music do you like to listen to?

J: I like every kind of music, but I do like classical music very, very much indeed. I was brought up on classical music. And so I love Bach and the Brandenburg. I love Mozart. I love opera. I love chamber music. And our daughter makes me go through the alphabet with pop groups. I don't know what they do or sing, but, I, I am able to go through the pop, the alphabet of pop groups, though I'm not much up-to-date at the moment.

I: Judi, I'm very grateful. Many thanks.

J: Thank you – thank you very much indeed.

# Key

## SPEAKING 1

### Things people like

1
2 clothes
3 music
4 animals
5 books
6 hobbies (e.g. photography)

## READING

**1**

Listening to music; cats; actors who are also good comedians; police programmes on the television; reading comics; going on holiday to Jamaica

**2**

Expensive shoe shops which don't have shoes in his size; violence; the idea of nuclear war; being misquoted in newspapers; racist jokes; rude people; Australian soap operas

## VOCABULARY

### Likes and dislikes: adjectives

**1**

*Very good*: fantastic; brilliant; terrific; great; wonderful; superb
*Very bad*: awful; dreadful

## 2

**bril**liant; ter**rific**; **aw**ful; **great**; **dread**ful; **won**derful; su**perb**

## 3

He thinks some comics are brilliant.
He thinks Stevie Wonder's early music is terrific.
He thinks it's awful when expensive shoe shops don't have shoes in his size.
He thinks Peter Sellers was great in the *Pink Panther* films.
He thinks Australian soap operas are dreadful.
He thinks *Police Squad* and *Hill Street Blues* are wonderful.
In his opinion his record collection is superb.

### Likes and dislikes: verbs

Most positive = *adore* → *be keen on* → *enjoy* / *be fond of* → *don't mind* → *hate* → *can't stand* / *detest* = Most negative

## GRAMMAR REVIEW 1

### Similarities and differences

### 1

b) 'Is she? I'm not.'
c) 'So do I.'
d) 'Neither do we.'
e) 'Do you? I don't.'

## PRONUNCIATION

### 1

Group A: sentences a), d) and e).
Group B: sentences b), c) and f).
Questions in which the pitch of the voice starts quite high often sound more friendly.

## LISTENING

### Listening

### 1

b) False   c) False   d) True   e) False

### 2

Judi's hobbies: b), e), f), g), j), l)

### 3

a) Drawing and painting.
b) Someone who likes plain, rather conventional food (meat and two vegetables).
c) Yes, because they share hobbies in common and spend their holidays together.

## GRAMMAR REVIEW 3

### The definite article (*the*)

### 1

Sentences a) and c) both have *the* in them because they refer to specific things. In b) Yugoslavia is a country which doesn't take *the*, and sentence d) is referring to things in general, not specific classical music.

### 2

a) My hobbies are reading ~~the~~ books and studying ~~the~~ languages. I like the Spanish lessons I'm having at the moment very much, but I'm finding the pronunciation and the grammar in Spanish really difficult.
b) The English food you get in the restaurants is often boring but in ~~the~~ private homes the cooking can be excellent. I usually like drinking ~~the~~ dry German wine with ~~the~~ meals, although I sometimes have ~~the~~ beer.
c) ~~The~~ animals are very important to English people, and they like ~~the~~ pets very much. However, some of the pets they keep are very strange.
d) My brother is very keen on ~~the~~ cars. He has to drive the models he sells, but according to him ~~the~~ Italian cars are the best.

### Direct and less direct questions

### 1

Questions a) and c) are less direct, because they are more personal.

# How do I look?

## Students' Book

**General theme:** people.
**Unit topic:** clothes; appearance.

**READING:** a magazine article about Rachel, a church minister.
**LEARNING FOCUS:** deducing the meaning of vocabulary (grammar and context).

**GRAMMAR REVIEW:** revision of present habits and routines (Present Simple, frequency adverbs/phrases); talking about present events (Present Continuous).
**PRONUNCIATION:** present tense endings (/s/, /z/ and /ɪz/); linking in connected speech (Present Simple/Continuous).
**SPEAKING 1:** appropriate language for different situations.
**WRITING:** punctuation.

**LISTENING:** vocabulary of clothes; describing appearances; people talking about their clothes.
**SPEAKING 2:** discussion of appropriate clothes for different situations.

## Workbook

**VOCABULARY:** clothes; parts of speech; jobs; names and titles.
**GRAMMAR:** Present Simple versus Present Continuous; frequency phrases and adverbs.
**WRITING:** punctuation; dictation.

## Language

This unit contrasts the Present Simple (for present habits, states and routines) and the Present Continuous (to talk about temporary present activity in progress). With the Present Continuous some Ts like to distinguish between talking about an activity at the moment of speaking (e.g. *Look! He's getting out of the car.*) and a temporary action or situation (e.g. *I'm learning Spanish*) not necessarily at that exact moment. In Unit 10 the Present Continuous is used to talk about the future.

## Common problems
### Present Simple

**1** In many languages (e.g. Spanish and Japanese) the Present Simple is commonly used to talk about the future (\**I give it to you tomorrow.*), whereas in English its use for future reference is restricted to fixed plans and time and conditional clauses (e.g. *if/when* clauses). Also in most languages (unlike English) it can be used to talk about time up to the moment of speaking (\**I work here four years now.*). Note that in Turkish and Arabic there is no independent verb *be* (\**My father teacher.*).

**2** Learners often omit the third person *-(e)s* from the third person singular, partly because it is the only inflection in English, partly because many languages (e.g. Danish and Thai) have no such inflected form. The spelling and the pronunciation of the third person also cause problems (see the *Language reference*).

**3** In negatives and question forms (see Review Unit 1) SS often confuse *do* and *does* and are unclear about what they mean (\**He no come.*).

**4** The position of adverbs of frequency in a sentence (\**Always I get home at 6 o'clock.* \**I once a year go to the dentist.*).

## Present Continuous

**1**  In some languages (e.g. Arabic, German and Greek) there is no Present Continuous form and so speakers of these languages tend to over-use the Present Simple.

**2**  'State' verbs (e.g. *like*, *think*, etc.) are a difficult 'concept' to grasp. As they do not normally take the continuous form, a common error is: e.g. *\*I am believing you.*

**3**  Spelling and pronunciation (see the *Language reference*). Also difficult for some SS (e.g. Spanish speakers) is the pronunciation of *-ing*, the consonant clusters *isn't/aren't* and hearing the contracted *is* in e.g. *He's sleeping*.

**4**  The word order of questions (e.g. *\*Where she is hiding? \*Is hiding she?*).

The Present Simple and Present Continuous are very common and very important verb forms. SS may think they 'know' them because they have done them before but they rarely use them with total accuracy at this level and still need a lot of practice.

In communication SS will be required to choose between the Present Simple and the Present Continuous. As few SS will be able to use a direct translation from their own language to help them, it is useful if they think of the Present Continuous as an 'aspect' of the Present tense and not as a separate tense (i.e. it doesn't separate present time from past time as the tense does; rather it describes the way we look at the action/state in terms of the passing of time). To contrast the two, the Present Continuous refers to temporary happenings in progress in the present, while the Present Simple describes longer states/habits.

## Punctuation

Notice that punctuation marks are used differently in many other languages. In Thai, for example, there are no punctuation marks at all since spaces between words indicate pauses. However, in most languages variations are relatively minor (e.g. in Greek the question mark is the same as the English semi-colon; in Italian small letters are used at the beginning of days and months; and in German and Danish there is a comma before reported speech).

# READING

## Before reading

PW (or as a class). Use the picture to get SS to predict and share opinions about:
a)  Rachel's job (she is a woman deacon)
b)  her personality
Ask them how they know. (There are many clues: e.g. her 'dog collar', the altar, the candles, etc. show she works in a church; and her short skirt makes her an unconventional minister.) Get SS to guess the 'answers' but don't give the game away. Instead let them check their answers in the *Reading*.

## Reading

● **Exercise 1**  Skimming exercise to determine the general content of what Rachel does/doesn't talk about. Possibly give time limit (two minutes?) for the reading and discourage use of dictionaries at this stage.

Note that some SS might be surprised (even shocked) that a woman is in a high position in the Church. You might want to point out that even today it is not very common in Britain. (This is suggested in paragraph 8.) It might be worth mentioning, too, that Rachel's humour (e.g. calling her cat 'Satan'), her badge, her colloquial language (e.g. 'had a gallon of black coffee') and her informal relationship with God, while cheeky, would probably not be regarded as offensive in 20th century Britain. Note the use of the Present Simple and frequency adverbs in the text.

● **Exercise 2**  The True/False statements (in the Present Simple) require more detailed reading. Correcting the incorrect statements makes the exercise more demanding. (Note that if you wish to use all the 'Guessing meaning' activities on SB pages 12 and 13 perhaps stop the students using their dictionaries during this exercise.) Follow-up could be done across the class to give practice of short answers (e.g. *Does she live alone? Yes, she does.*).

● **Exercise 3**  GW. More interpretative questions.

● **Exercise 4**  PW/GW. Encourages SS to explore the text for the use of frequency adverbs and to work out a rule for their position in a sentence. Encourage SS to check their ideas with the *Language reference*.

● **Exercise 5** In this discussion about our image of a typical minister possibly make something of stereotyping in traditional male/female roles. Ask whether it is possible to be both informal and serious in such a job.

# LEARNING FOCUS

## Guessing meaning

The introduction to this exercise explains how the meaning of a word can be deduced from both its grammatical function and the context. The exercise lays the foundation for one of the ways SS should be encouraged to deal with unknown words in texts throughout the course. You might find it worthwhile to refer them back to this exercise from later units when they get stuck.

● **Exercises 1–3** Don't let SS look the words up in their dictionaries until they have done the exercises.

● **Exercise 4** Possibly ask SS to make a note of five useful words they would like to remember and share them in groups or with you. Introduce the idea to SS that while some words they will probably only need to recognise, others they will want to use. Encourage them to begin to take responsibility for managing their vocabulary lists. (There is specific help in Review Units 3 and 4.)

# GRAMMAR REVIEW

## Present habits and routines

● **Exercises 1–3** On the position of frequency adverbs in Present Simple sentences make the link with Exercise 4 in the *Reading*. Possibly point out that the order is not the same after the verb *be* and modals (*He is **always** late. I will **often** be late.*). The exercises give further practice of the Present Simple, including revision of the question form practised in Review Unit 1. Possibly refer SS to the *Language reference* either before or after these exercises.

● **Exercise 2** Encourage SS to use short answers (*Yes, I do.*). Allow SS A and B to swap roles.

● **Exercise 3** Possibly get SS to find out more things about each other that they didn't discover in Review Unit 1 (e.g. *What do you do in the evenings?*).

## Talking about present events

● **Exercise 1** Designed to help SS share what they know about the use of the Present Continuous.

● **Exercise 2** PW/GW. Focuses on the form (including spelling) of the Present Continuous in an extended context (which helps reinforce its use). Students should skim-read what Clare says and get an idea of what is going on. Don't give away the context (i.e. daughter talking to mother on the phone): let SS guess. (Later, in Exercise 3, they can check their guesses by listening to the recording.) Use the exercise to reinforce the spelling rules outlined in the *Language reference*, Section 4.

● **Exercise 3** Possibly feed back guesses on to an OHT / the board before listening, and then pause the tape to check answers.

● **Exercise 4** Use item c) to practise Present Continuous question forms.

● **Exercise 5** PW/GW. Possibly practise contrastive stress (e.g. *They're **not** watering the plants. The plants are **dying**.*).

## Simple or Continuous?

Note that 'state' verbs (see the *Language reference*, Section 5) are not normally used in the continuous. There is a further exercise in the WB. Possibly elicit examples for those state verbs that sometimes take the continuous (e.g. *I'm **having** a bath. / I **have** a car.*).

# PRONUNCIATION

## Present Simple and Continuous

● **Exercise 1** The 'rule' for Present Simple endings is given in the *Language reference*, Section 3. SS will need to hear the difference between 'voiced' and 'unvoiced' sounds (see also Unit 15). Possibly sensitise them by getting them to turn on and off the 'voicing' of the /s/ and /z/ sounds while they have their hand on the outside of the

throat or their hands over their ears
(/sssssssszzzzzzzzzzzsssss/ etc.). Try to get SS
to predict their answers from the rule before they
check with the recording (not an easy task).

● **Exercise 2** Practises distinguishing sounds
linked together in connected speech in Present
Continuous / Present Simple sentences. Item a) is
a way-in to the more difficult dictation task in
item b).

# SPEAKING 1

## Social situations

'Free-standing' exercise to sensitise SS to the need
to choose appropriate language for a situation. For
many of these language 'functions' (e.g. asking for
permission, introducing someone) there are a
number of possible expressions. When SS report
back, compare their answers for such things as
accuracy, naturalness and formality/informality.
Elicit corrections for errors. A particularly useful
exercise for any student taking the ARELS oral
exam and anyone living in or going to Britain.

# WRITING

## Punctuation

● **Exercise 1** PW/GW before looking at the rules
on SB page 150.

● **Exercise 2** Use photograph of Princess Diana
to establish the context of the passage (e.g. *'What
kind of person do you think Princess Diana is? Do
you think she is a very formal person with her
friends? Does she have a sense of humour? What
kind of food does she like to eat?'*).

If SS are still having problems, give the exercise
in the WB for homework. In future written
exercises pay attention to punctuation. You might
need to refer them back to the rules and get them
to compile their own example sentences which
they could keep for reference.

# LISTENING

## Vocabulary: clothes

Aims to warm-up SS to the theme of the *Listening*
and to activate clothes vocabulary. As a lead-in
possibly ask SS to describe someone's clothes (in
the class?) and let other SS guess who it is. This
will provide revision of the Present Continuous.
(Note there is a further exercise on clothes
vocabulary in the WB.)

## Before listening

● **Exercises 1 and 2** Prediction linked to the
*Listening*. Useful language could be: *She looks/
seems …*

● **Exercises 3 and 4** Personalised discussion.
Omit if you prefer to go straight into the *Listening*.
Exercise 4 practises the Present Simple/Continuous
contrast.

## Listening

● **Exercise 1** PW/GW. Break up text and get SS
to do the exercise after each speaker? You need
not elicit answers until the end. Useful vocabulary:
*stripy, spotty, leather, not bothered*.

● **Exercises 2 and 3** Possibly get SS to follow the
tapescript (full edition of the SB only) on this
occasion and check their answers to Exercise 1
above at the same time. Before doing Exercise 3
elicit the clothes vocabulary from the pictures.

# SPEAKING 2

## Group report

How people choose to dress in different situations
tells us about both the people and the situation. In
a multinational class this exercise could lead to a
discussion of the different conventions and
expectations in different cultures. Possibly, see
which people like to break with convention and
how.

● **Exercises 1 and 2** If SS want to use the
vocabulary practised above, fine, but don't force it.
If there are language errors, note them for
discussion later but don't interrupt the flow of
ideas.

# Tapescripts

## RECORDING 1

'... Hi!... Yes, it's Clare... We're OK... Yes, of course we're watering the plants... Oh, they're fine... No, the house isn't a mess – one of us is cleaning it every day... Yes, I loved the dress... No, really! I'm wearing it at the moment, actually. Are you having a good time?... Oh, great!... David? Oh, I expect he's doing his homework in his room... Yes, the dog's fine, too... Of course, we're not forgetting to feed him. What do you think we are?!... Yes, I know he's not allowed in the sitting room – we're keeping him in his basket in the hall... No, we're not eating junk food. Pauline is cooking at this very moment... Oh, I can't remember. Chicken, I think. OK, give Dad our love. See you soon... What?... Tomorrow! Well, why are you asking me all these questions then?!'

## RECORDING 2

a) works
b) loses
c) goes
d) drives
e) gets
f) watches
g) knows
h) starts
i) dances

## RECORDING 3

1) How do you do?
2) What are you reading?
3) Where do you come from?
4) Why is she looking out of the window?
5) How often does she go swimming?
6) Where are you working at the moment?

## RECORDING 4

ANNIE: I like wearing the kind of clothes that I know my mother doesn't wear. I like, I like to look young and I like wearing bright colours and things that stand out in a crowd like, I like leather trousers and skirts, I like bright, bright colours, in my hair as well – like slides and things but also I dye my hair quite often. I don't see why I should look like everyone else in the street. It's fun. Clothes should be fun not something really serious. I could never spend, I don't know, £100 on a skirt for example. It's just such a waste of money.

SARA: I mean, I like dressing up sometimes, but most of the time I actually feel uncomfortable, especially for my job 'cause I, I teach and, you know, if I'm wearing a skirt or a blouse I go in and I feel as if I'm teaching really formally and stiffly just because of what I'm wearing, so I tend to like to wear, you know, I like wearing sort of stripy things and spotty things and, and bright bouncy things really, and I'm not really bothered about the fashion. So I just like to wear the sort of things, you know, that like I feel comfortable in.

LIZ: I like wearing quite smart clothes because I feel better that way. I like to feel that I'm presenting the right image because I come into work – I work in an office –
and I feel that people need to have some respect for me. They're going to do that more if I'm dressed to look as if I have some control over my situation and everything else. I enjoy wearing these clothes and I therefore feel more comfortable in them, which is also an additional part of it. At the present moment I, I'm wearing a suit and, and a shirt and high heels, but that is not because I have to. It's because I actually feel better that way and that the image that I'm presenting will give people more confidence.

MIKE: Yes, well it's because I work in a bank really. I'm expected to wear formal clothes, pinstripe suit, tie, dark shoes, usually. Other times I do wear other, other sorts of clothes but I, I quite like wearing things like that. We're a bit of an old-fashioned firm and they, they insist that we do.

# Key

## READING

### Reading

**1**
c) and e)

**2**
a) False. She finds it difficult to get up in the mornings.
b) True.
c) False. She eats yoghurt and fruit for lunch and in the evening eats something from the freezer which she cooks in the microwave.
d) True.
e) False. She is not at all maternal.
f) False. She used to have a black cat which died last year.

**3**
a) *He* is God. In English the personal pronoun when talking about God usually begins with a capital letter even when it is not at the beginning of a sentence.
b) No, this is an exaggeration. She means she drinks a lot.
c) She is working at a college.
d) She relaxes by playing the piano, walking, doing yoga, reading, seeing friends and watching television.
e) We see examples of her sense of humour in her exaggerations ('a gallon of black coffee and 200 cigarettes'), the badge she wears on her handbag, the name of her black cat ('Satan'), and her jokes about stealing babies from supermarkets and having to find a wealthy man.
f) No, she doesn't earn a lot. Ministers, she says, earn only £7,500 a year, so she jokes that she will have to find herself a wealthy man.
g) Yes, because some people don't approve of women working in the Church.

**4**

a) 'My first waking thought is *usually* along the lines ...'
   (paragraph 1)
   'I *often* think it would be nice ...' (paragraph 2)
   '*Most mornings* I wash my hair ...' (paragraph 6)
   'on the move, *usually* on my way to talk ...'
   (paragraph 9)
   'I *usually* get home around 5 p.m.' (paragraph 10)
   '*Sometimes* I have a bath and read ...' (paragraph 10)
   '*mostly* with friends ...' (paragraph 10)
   'I *occasionally* just slump into a chair ...' (paragraph 10)
   'I do *sometimes* miss my black cat.' (paragraph 10)

b) In the majority of cases the adverb comes after the
   subject and before the main verb ('I *usually* get ...').
   They come after the verb *be* ('... is *usually* along the
   lines') and the auxiliary *do* ('I do *sometimes* miss ...').
   The adverb *sometimes* can come at the beginning of a
   phrase or sentence ('*Sometimes* I miss ...').

## LEARNING FOCUS

### Guessing meaning

**1**

a) noun
b) adjective
c) verb
d) verb
e) adverb
f) adjective

**2**

a) *unserious and not proper*: It comes after the verb *be*
   and modifying phrase *a bit*, so it is obviously an
   adjective. The meaning is suggested by the joke on the
   badge – slightly shocking when worn by a woman in
   the Church?

b) *have a good opinion of*: The auxiliary *don't* suggests a
   main verb. The phrase *keep out of their way* in the
   sentence following suggests negative views.

c) *relax*: We can work out the meaning from the examples
   which follow.

d) *have feelings like a mother*: Links with the idea of
   marriage in the previous sentence and the joke about
   stealing babies from supermarkets in the rest of this
   sentence.

e) *very rich*: Comes after the verb *be* and before a noun. It
   obviously describes a man and is connected with
   money. It can't mean *poor* because she is already poor.
   She needs money so the man must be rich.

**3**

They mean *put*.

## GRAMMAR REVIEW

### Talking about present events

**1**

Present Continuous (or Present Progressive).
It is used to talk about an activity, temporary action or
situation in progress in the present. It is also used for
future plans and personal arrangements (see Unit 10).

**2**

2  cleaning
3  wearing
4  having
5  doing
6  forgetting
7  keeping
8  eating
9  cooking
10 asking

**4**

a) Clare is talking to her mother.

b) Her mother and father have gone away and to Clare's
   surprise they are coming back tomorrow. Clare and the
   others have been told to do a number of things, like
   water the plants, which they haven't done. Clare is
   pretending that she and her brother, David, and sister,
   Pauline, have done as they've been asked.

c) Possible questions etc.:
   'Hello, darling. Is that you?'
   'How are you?'
   'Are you watering the plants?'
   'How are the others?'
   'I suppose the house is a mess, isn't it?'
   'Did you like the dress I bought you?'
   'You're just saying that, aren't you?'
   ('Yes, excellent.')
   'Where's David? What's he doing?'
   'Is the dog OK?'
   'I bet you're forgetting to feed him, aren't you?'
   'You do remember that we don't like him in the sitting
   room, don't you?'
   'You're not eating that awful junk food, are you?'
   'What's she cooking?'
   ('We're coming home tomorrow.')
   ('I said, we're coming home tomorrow.')

**5**

The plants are dying. The house is dirty and untidy. Clare
is not wearing a dress. David is not doing his homework in
his room. The dog is not in his basket in the hall. Pauline is
eating a hamburger and she isn't cooking.

### Simple or Continuous?

**1**

Sentences b), d), f), g) are incorrect. They should be
Present Simple. In c) *think* is used correctly because it
describes an activity rather than a state of mind. Verbs
which describe states rather than actions do not normally
have a continuous form.

## PRONUNCIATION

### Present Simple and Continuous

**1**

a) /s/: works, gets, starts
/z/: goes, drives, knows
/ɪz/: loses, watches, dances

**2**

a) How do you do? (*4 words*)
b) What are you reading? (*4 words*)
c) Where do you come from? (*5 words*)
d) Why is she looking out of the window? (*8 words*)
e) How often does she go swimming? (*6 words*)
f) Where are you working at the moment? (*7 words*)

## SPEAKING 1

### Social situations

**1**

Example answers:

a) Excuse me, Phil. Could you tell me what the word *pray* means?
b) Sorry, Sarah. I've got a problem. How do you spell *photograph*?
c) I'm terribly sorry. I couldn't get a taxi anywhere.
d) Sorry. Could I ask you something? I don't know how to pronounce this word. Sorry to interrupt.
e) I don't know how to put this, but I've got a problem. My brother's having a party and he wants me to help. Do you think I could possibly leave a bit early?
f) Carlos, I want you to meet a good friend of mine. Anne-Marie this is Carlos. Carlos, Anne-Marie.
g) Oh, that's OK. Forget it. No problem.
h) Great. Well done! I'm really jealous.
i) You fool! I told you you needed to work for that exam. You were never very good at French.

## WRITING

### Punctuation

**1**

1 d)  2 e)  3 g)  4 f)  5 a)  6 h)  7 b)  8 c)

**2**

How do the rich and famous spend their lives? The answers are sometimes surprising! At Princess Diana's private parties, for example, there are no cooks or servants – the food provided is simple pasta and salad – and the conversation is relaxed and lively. She and her friends like to laugh at the latest pictures of her in the newspaper, talk about her latest dresses or examine her new shoes. They also like to gossip about friends and tell plenty of jokes. Typical Diana expressions on these occasions are 'I just don't believe it!' and 'That sounds like fun!'

## LISTENING

### Vocabulary: clothes

1 suit, waistcoat, shirt, tie
2 jumper
3 tights, blouse, high heels
4 jacket, training shoes, T-shirt
5 boots, shirt
6 tights, leather skirt, high heels

### Listening

**1**

*Annie:* a) Yes  b) No
*Sara:* a) No  b) No
*Liz:* a) Yes  b) No
*Mike:* a) Yes  b) Yes

**2**

a) *Annie:* 6  *Sara:* 2?  *Liz:* 3  *Mike:* 1
b) *Annie:* Likes to look young, wear bright colours. Likes to stand out in a crowd. Likes leather. Likes clothes to be fun, but doesn't like spending a lot of money on them.
*Sara:* Doesn't like dressing up very often. Likes to dress informally and comfortably. Not bothered about fashion but likes bright, stripy and spotty things.
*Liz:* Likes wearing smart clothes. Conscious of image, wants to create respect and confidence in others.
*Mike:* Quite likes formal clothes.

**3**

Tracksuit, T-shirt, raincoat, pullover, dress

# Foreign adventures

## Students' Book

**General theme:** living abroad.
**Unit topic:** adventures abroad.

**LISTENING:** an anecdote about a kidnapping experience.
**LEARNING FOCUS 1:** using a monolingual dictionary (to find the meaning and pronunciation of words).
**VOCABULARY:** guessing meaning from context; nationality words.

**GRAMMAR REVIEW:** regular and irregular Past Simple forms; question forms using the Past Simple; Past Simple or *used to*; Past Simple or Past Continuous; time expressions (e.g. *ago*, *last*).
**PRONUNCIATION:** Past Simple endings (/t/, /d/, /ɪd/); Past Continuous (weak forms of *was* and *were*).

**LEARNING FOCUS 2:** keeping vocabulary records.
**SPEAKING:** 'ranking' activity (a walking holiday in Thailand); functional expressions (making suggestions, giving opinions, agreeing/disagreeing).
**WRITING:** identifying linking expressions (addition, time and contrast) in a text; writing a story based on a sound sequence.

## Workbook

**READING:** newspaper text on an earthquake ordeal; associated question forms and vocabulary in context.
**GRAMMAR:** time expressions; *used to*; irregular Past Simple forms; pronunciation of Past Simple endings; past forms and linkers.
**VOCABULARY:** countries and nationalities; family relationships; spelling.

## Language

The language focus of this unit is on ways of talking about the past. This includes regular and irregular Past Simple forms, the Past Continuous, and *used to*. Emphasis in this unit is on the contrast between these past forms, and their pronunciation. In Review Unit 4 the Past Simple will be contrasted with the Present Perfect for indefinite time. As in all the Review Units, it is expected that SS already 'know' the target language and need more practice, revision and fine-tuning. As a result, they are 'thrown into' an activity first, rather than having the target language re-presented. However, past tenses are frequently a problem, even for SS at this level.

## Common problems
### Past Simple

**1**   In place of the Past Simple many languages (e.g. German, Italian) can use the Present Perfect (*have* + past participle) to talk about a completed action.

**2**   SS often avoid using *Did* in question forms, preferring to use the affirmative form (see Review Unit 1 in relation to the Present Simple).

**3**   Many SS find the voiced/unvoiced (and /ɪd/) endings difficult to distinguish and produce (see the *Language reference*).

**4**   The irregular forms still need frequent revision (see SB page 148).

### Past Continuous

**1**   The Past Continuous can cause problems because SS often want to use it for completed activities (e.g. *When I was a child I was living in Sheffield.*) rather than activities in progress which are not complete at the time we are thinking about.

**2**   For the same reason (i.e. misunderstanding the focus on duration) SS often find the difference between the following two question forms difficult to understand: *What were you doing?* (e.g. at the time you heard the noise); *What did you do?* (afterwards).

**3** SS need to be reminded that some verbs do not take the continuous form (see the *Language reference* in Review Unit 2).

**4** SS often use *was* and *were* in their 'strong' forms.

### Used to

**1** *Used to* is often confused with *be used to* (**I am used to live in the USA.*) and *use* (*I used a knife to cut it.*) because SS find it difficult to understand that *used to* exists only in the past. They also need to be reminded that it refers to discontinued habitual actions and states – not single actions (see the *Language reference*).

**2** The form of this structure is difficult because it doesn't obey the 'rules' of other verbs. Students often find the question form (*Did you use to?* or, less commonly, *Used you to?*) and the negative form (*I didn't use to* or *I usedn't to*) a problem.

**3** The pronunciation is also confusing. *Used to* is pronounced /juːst ə / with /s/ whereas *use* (e.g. *I **use** a word-processor to write with.*) is pronounced /juːz/ with /z/.

**4** *To* in *used to* is usually pronounced weakly (/tə/) in normal connected speech, although not in short answers.

## LISTENING

### Before listening

● **Exercises 1 and 2**   PW. Explain the word *kidnapping*, possibly by reference to a recent event in your own country. Be sensitive to any painful events in SS' own country and make it clear that kidnappings happen all over the world – not only in the Third World. Try to elicit political as well as financial motives, and develop into a class discussion. You might also want to teach *ransom, hostages, rebel* and (because it comes up in the listening text) *release*.

● **Exercise 3**   The aim is not only to introduce vocabulary and information necessary for the listening activity but also to give SS a purpose for listening, and to motivate them. Feedback from the different groups should be encouraged, and the new vocabulary elicited or introduced and put on the board. Tell SS that this is a true story.

### Listening

● **Exercise 1**   Encourage SS to listen only for gist, to get the general storyline. SS might possibly be able to have a go at Exercise 2, which requires slightly more detailed information, before a further listening. Notice that the recording contains many uses of the Past Simple, the Past Continuous, the Past Perfect and *used to*.

● **Exercise 3**   SS should work individually and then in pairs to try and correct the text. Then play the tape a second or third time so that they can check their answers. Possibly, in a 'whole-class' situation, get SS to ask for the tape to be stopped when they hear an answer. In the feedback you could encourage them to use contrastive stress: e.g. '*No, they weren't **Australian**. They were **American**.*'

● **Exercise 4**   As SS reconstruct their story see how well they use past forms. Encourage them to use *used to* in items f) and g) if they don't do so without prompting. Elicit answers from different pairs and put them on the board or on an OHT. (Alternatively, if there is time, get SS to write up the sentences themselves.) Encourage the rest of the class to suggest improvements. This would obviously be an opportunity to give 'input' into the uses and forms of the past forms, and you might like to go directly to the GRAMMAR REVIEW. Refer SS to the *Language reference*.

As a follow-up SS could be asked to talk about any strange or frightening experiences they have had abroad or at home.

## LEARNING FOCUS 1

### Using a monolingual dictionary

This section introduces SS to using a monolingual dictionary. Possibly recommend a specific one which you keep copies of in the classroom, or, alternatively, give them a choice of a number of different dictionaries. If regular use of a monolingual dictionary can be built into classroom practice SS will soon learn to develop very useful dictionary skills and become more independent learners. Stress that there is still a place for good bilingual dictionaries, but that it is not always possible to find the information they need in these, particularly as they become more advanced.

To make the activities more fun SS can be given a time limit and could work in pairs.

● **Exercise 2**   A good opportunity to introduce the use of the phonemic chart in the coursebook (see SB page 149) and point out the differences between normal spelling and the phonemic symbols. Get SS to use this chart to interpret the symbols in the dictionary. Regular reference to a phonemic chart in the classroom will also help SS to become accustomed to the symbols, although it is not necessary for most SS to learn them by heart. You might like to point out that there are two possible pronunciations of the word *mask* (see dictionary entry): in some parts of the English speaking world (e.g. northern England) it is pronounced /mæsk/.

● **Exercise 3**   Point out that there are different headwords for *rush* and that SS have to refer closely to the context to find out which of the meanings is relevant to them. Get them to tell you how the word is pronounced.

You might want to do extra practice on areas such as finding definitions and working out pronunciation in future lessons. A useful book for this is *Longman Dictionary Skills Handbook.*

# VOCABULARY

## Guessing meaning

Encourage SS to make intelligent guesses and then tell them to use a dictionary to check their predictions. This is a good opportunity to talk to them about how they might use the *Tapescripts* (full edition of the SB only) – as follow-up to work done in class, for example.

## Nationality words

Reference has already been made in this unit to *Sri Lanka* and *Americans.* Make sure SS realise that the definite article is not usually used for countries (except for groups of islands or states such as *the USA, the USSR, the Seychelles*, etc.), and that capital letters are used at the beginning of names of countries and nationalities. The dictionary could be used to check the stressed syllable. There is more work on this in the WB if you require class supplementation.

● **Exercise 2**   Could be done either as a class activity in teams or as group activities.

# GRAMMAR REVIEW

## Past Simple

● **Exercises 1 and 2**   The first reading of the text is mainly for comprehension. (SS might need some persuading to ignore the gaps at first.) Before they read, help SS to predict what the article is about, by explaining or eliciting the meaning of words in the title (e.g. *ordeal, seaweed*) and using the photo as a lead-in. You could elicit some of the vocabulary in the article in advance (e.g. *Why do you think the family were drifting?* to elicit *run out of petrol*). You may need to explain *outboard motor, bloody awful,* and *urine.*

Highlight *used to / didn't use to* in the last two paragraphs, and the word *nightmare,* previously introduced in the *Listening.*

● **Exercises 3 and 4**   PW/GW? Focus on regular and irregular past forms, (see also PRONUNCIATION). Note the change in spellings of regular verbs such as *carry* and *try.* Draw SS' attention to the irregular verbs chart on SB page 148.

● **Exercise 5**   Prepare SS by giving B some time to think of questions (all the Bs in the class could work together to do this) and A time to read the article again. Probably a good idea to try out one or two questions first in front of the class, and perhaps do some remedial work on question forms. SS will probably have problems with use of the different auxiliaries *Did, was/were,* and with the question *What was the weather like?* (practised in Unit 7). If there is time, this could develop into a roleplay, possibly to be recorded on audio or video tape. Feedback provides a focus for remedial work on question forms in the past.

## Past Simple or *used to*?

● **Exercise 1**   Discussion should focus on both the use and form of *used to.* Possibly contrast it with *to be used to* + *-ing* and *use* if SS are having problems (and if you think it will not confuse them too much). Focus SS' attention on the weak form of *to* in *used to.*

● **Exercise 2**   PW discussion before getting feedback as a class. Give some examples first.

## Past Simple or Past Continuous?

● **Exercise 1** Encourage discussion of the reasons why one alternative is better than another. There is practice of the weak form of *was* and *were* in the PRONUNCIATION section.

● **Exercise 2** Practises the difference between *while* and *when*. Make it clear that they can usually come either at the beginning or in the middle of the sentence.

● **Exercise 3** Focuses on the difference between what you were doing when something happened (i.e. activity in progress), which is practised in the previous exercise, and what you did next (a specific event) – a difficult 'concept' for many SS.

## Time expressions

● **Exercise 1** An opportunity to do some work on linkage and elision in connected speech (*last Friday* /lɑːsˈfraɪdɪ/, *for ages*, etc.). There is more work on this in the WB.

● **Exercise 2** Point out how we write *5th May* but we say *'on the 5th of May'*. The activities 'The answers' in *Grammar in Action* or 'Our lives' in *Grammar Games* (see *Bibliography*) fit in well here as an alternative. (SS write on sticky labels various dates which are important to them. They then ask each other or explain to each other the significance of these dates.)

# PRONUNCIATION

## Past Simple

● **Exercise 1** These words can be read instead of played on tape. Show SS the difference between voiced and unvoiced consonants and get SS to try making the sounds themselves (see Review Unit 2 and Unit 15). Since SS are working the rule out for themselves you may need to give clues, e.g. by exaggerating the difference between /t/ and /d/.

## Past Continuous

Try to give SS a sense of the rhythm of English by showing them the words which are stressed and those which are weak. This is focused on more in Units 6 and 13.

# LEARNING FOCUS 2

## Keeping vocabulary records

### Remembering what words mean

● **Exercises 1 and 2** SS will probably be familiar with many of the abbreviations by now from their dictionary work, but you could show SS how to look up abbreviations in the dictionary.

● **Exercise 3** Could develop into a useful discussion on why it is a good idea to keep vocabulary records and other ways of recording new words (e.g. *'spidergrams'* or *'networks'* such as the following).

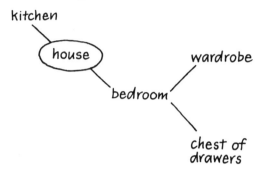

### Organising a vocabulary notebook

● **Exercise 1** Could develop into a useful discussion on what is important vocabulary, and the difference between active and passive vocabulary, with comments from you.

For the future encourage SS to jot down vocabulary during lessons and check their vocabulary books and/or the organisation of their files from time to time.

# SPEAKING

Make sure SS understand the situation before they start Exercises 1 and 2. Check that they understand the vocabulary. Small pictures or flashcards may come in handy. Use the photo in the book to set or elicit the context. Perhaps find out if anyone in the class has ever been on this kind of holiday.

● **Exercise 1** Make it clear that SS must select only *ten* items (no more, no less). The discussion on what to take could be built up in a 'pyramid' fashion until every group agrees, but this can be very time-consuming! Alternatively do it in groups and get each group to report back to the class, justifying their decisions.

• **Exercise 2**  You may prefer to elicit these expressions from the SS and put them on the board before beginning the discussion. Get SS to suggest others, and practise the intonation.

# WRITING

## Linking expressions

• **Exercise 1**  Possibly check the basic details of the story first by asking questions about where Shell went and why, why he didn't have a guide, who he went up with, who Esther was, etc. (as open questions or true/false questions).

• **Exercise 2**  Make sure that SS know what linking expressions are (by writing two sentences and asking them to make one sentence from them). Then explain the three different categories of linkers by putting three sentences on the board and eliciting the meaning of each linker (i.e. *addition*, *time* and *contrast*) before asking SS to underline and group the linkers in the text. After the grouping activities it may be necessary to exemplify the meaning of linking words which the SS didn't understand. Examples:
*I bought some bread **and** cheese.* (addition)
**As soon as** *he finished he went home.* (time)
*He ate the bread **but** not the cheese.* (contrast)

Note that linking expressions also come up in Units 6, 8 and 17. Emphasise their importance in clear organised writing, and point out that linking expressions connect ideas *across* sentences as well as *within* sentences. (There is more work on this in Unit 8.) Point out the reference section on *Linking expressions* on SB page 150.

• **Exercise 3**  The first activity is speaking. The story could be done in pairs or groups or as a 'chain story', with one student writing a line of the story and passing it to another member of the group until it's finished.

In future get SS to check their own and/or their partner's work for accurate use of language just studied. Refer them to the punctuation chart on SB page 150 and remind them to check for past forms and linking expressions too.

# Tapescripts

## RECORDING 1

When I lived in Sri Lanka I lived in a town called Jaffna, in the north of the island, and I had two American friends who lived next door to me. And they were sitting at home one evening watching a video, and they were in their bedroom – and that was the only air-conditioned room in the house – and there was a knock at the door, and Stan went to answer the door and some boys came to the door, and they were asking for money for the rebuilding of the local library. And he didn't believe them, and he sent them away and he shut the door and went back into the bedroom. Just as he'd got back into the bedroom, suddenly there was a big noise, the door was broken down and four or five masked men rushed into the room carrying guns, and shouting at them. And they tied them up – they took hold of their hands and tied them behind their backs and pushed them around quite a lot. They put blindfolds on both of them and took them outside and pushed them into a van and drove them around for quite a long time, and took them off to some remote part of the island.

And all this happened while I was waiting for them in a hotel in Kandy because we had planned to send, to spend some time together – it was a holiday weekend. And, in fact, they'd been kidnapped by some extremists who were trying to, trying to get autonomy from other parts of the island. And they were kept for a week. They were kidnapped and kept for a week. And after that eventually they were released. They were very well treated overall but it wasn't a very pleasant experience. And after they were released they told us the story – they told us everything that happened to them. This was just before they were sent back to America.

And I saw them again about a year later, and they told me that even, even then – this was a year after it happened – they still were both very security-conscious, -conscious and they used to get up in the middle of the night and check all the doors and windows and they used to both suffer from terrible nightmares. And I think it still happens to them. A very difficult experience to get over.

## RECORDING 2

asked, arrived, started

a) asked  b) tasted  c) retired  d) drifted  e) appeared
f) talked  g) tried  h) waited

## RECORDING 3

MAN:  'He was driving too fast.'
WOMAN: 'Was he?'

## RECORDING 4

a) I was eating my lunch when he arrived.
b) Was it an accident, or did he do it on purpose?
c) While they were playing football they broke a window.
d) I'm not sure, but I think they were.
e) It wasn't possible to fly there direct.
f) She was having a drink when he arrived.

## RECORDING 5

[Sound story: see Key.]

# Key

## LISTENING

### Listening

**2**
a) American.
b) As hostages. The kidnappers were trying to get autonomy from other parts of the island.
c) To a remote part of the island.
d) They were released.

**3**
- The couple were American, not Australian.
- They were kept for a week, not a month.
- Their captors demanded autonomy, not large sums of money.
- The couple were watching a video, not having breakfast.
- There were four or five masked men, not two.
- The masked men didn't search the house at all.
- The couple didn't escape; they were released.
- They were very well treated by their captors; they didn't suffer badly at all.

**4**
a) The American couple were watching a video when there was a knock on the door.
b) Stanley sent the boys away, closed the door, and went back into the bedroom.
c) The men were wearing masks and carrying guns.
d) The men put blindfolds on them, pushed them into a van and took them away.
e) While this was happening, Sue was waiting at a hotel in Kandy.
f) For a long time after the kidnapping her friends used to check / checked their doors and windows at night.
g) They also used to have / had nightmares for some time afterwards.

## LEARNING FOCUS 1

### Using a monolingual dictionary

**1**
nouns: *men*, *room*
adjective: *masked*
preposition: *into*

**2**
a) *adj* (= adjective)

**3**
a) The first meaning (**rush**[1]).

## VOCABULARY

### Guessing meaning

**1**

a) ii)  b) i)  c) ii)  d) ii)  e) i)

## Nationality words

**1**

The word in the box is *RUSSIA*.

## GRAMMAR REVIEW

### Past Simple

**1**
a) Out at sea near Majorca.
b) They were on a pleasure trip, on their motorboat.
c) They ran out of petrol.
d) A Spanish fishing boat rescued them.

**2**
a) False  b) False  c) True  d) False  e) False

**3**
*Regular*: appear (appeared); taste (tasted); carry (carried); drift (drifted); try (tried)
*Irregular*: eat (ate); become (became); be (was/were); say (said); drink (drank)

**4**
1  ate
2  drifted
3  became
4  were
5  said
6  carried
7  tried
8  drank
9  tasted
10  appeared

### Past Simple or *used to*?

**1**
a), c) and f)

### Past Simple or Past Continuous?

**1**
a) stole; was swimming
b) met; was going out
c) was driving; made / was making
d) were living; happened
e) attacked; was walking
f) left; was shining; was raining

**2**
b) While we were flying over the sea I saw the left wing was on fire.
c) While I was doing aerobics I twisted my ankle.
d) While they were walking through the jungle Sue nearly stood on a snake.
e) He was having lunch with his boss when he spilt red wine over her white suit.
f) She was reading in bed when she heard a noise downstairs.
g) He was washing up when he broke her favourite vase.

## Time expressions

b) last, this, at
c) last, this, in, during
d) in, during
e) ago
f) last, this, in, during
g) during, at
h) in, during

# PRONUNCIATION

## Past Simple

**1**
a) asked /t/
b) tasted /ɪd/
c) retired /d/
d) drifted /ɪd/
e) appeared /d/
f) talked /t/
g) tried /d/
h) waited /ɪd/

## Past Continuous

**2**
a) I *was* eating my lunch … (*weak*)
b) *Was* it an accident … (*strong*)
c) While they *were* playing … (*weak*)
d) … I think they *were*. (*strong*)
e) It *wasn't* possible … (*strong*)
f) She *was* having a drink … (*weak*)

# LEARNING FOCUS 2

## Keeping vocabulary records

**1**
*noun* and *adjective*

**2**
a) vb (or v)   b) adv   c) prep   d) e.g.

**3**
She has translated the new word into her own language; she has defined or explained the word; she has written an example sentence using the word.

# WRITING

## Linking expressions

**1**
Example answer:
A young American man came to Sumatra to climb one of the volcanoes. As he couldn't find a guide, he did the climb on his own. Unfortunately he fell into the mouth of the volcano and nearly died.

Luckily the manager of his hotel became worried when he didn't return. With the help of a local spiritualist she found the man and he was eventually rescued by the police.

**2**
addition: *and, as well as, too*
time: *as soon as, before, when, while, later, finally, eventually*
contrast: *but, although, however*

**3**
Example story:
Last year, Francesca flew to Australia on a business trip. As soon as she arrived, she checked into her hotel.

While she was having a shower, the telephone rang. She turned off the shower and went to see who it was. It was the business colleague who she had come to Australia to see. He asked her to meet him at his office at six o'clock for an emergency meeting. She agreed to the meeting but she wasn't very pleased as she was tired after her long journey and had to rush if she was going to get there on time.

She got a taxi from outside the hotel, but unfortunately there was a lot of traffic on the winding road by the sea and the taxi driver drove very fast. Suddenly, a lorry came round a corner very quickly and crashed into the taxi. A few minutes later an ambulance arrived and took Francesca to hospital. She was seriously hurt and nearly died.

(Luckily, after a few weeks, she recovered and two months later, she returned to England. It had been a lucky escape!)

# Home thoughts from abroad

## Students' Book

**General theme:** living abroad.
**Unit topic:** living in Britain.

**READING:** two articles by foreigners living in Britain, an American man and a French woman.
**VOCABULARY:** deducing meaning from context; Americanisms.

**GRAMMAR REVIEW:** revision of Present Perfect (for result and experience or indefinite time) in contrast with Past Simple; time expressions (e.g. *already*, *yet*); question tags.
**PRONUNCIATION:** intonation in question tags; linking in connected speech (contracted forms of Present Perfect).

**LEARNING FOCUS:** keeping a grammar book; ways of learning English; learner diaries.
**WRITING:** spelling.

## Workbook

**LISTENING:** two British people talking about learning a foreign language; free writing on similar experiences.
**GRAMMAR:** Past Simple versus Present Perfect (including time expressions); *been* versus *gone*; question tags.
**VOCABULARY:** living in Britain (names of places in British English); names of places in American English.
**WRITING:** dictation.

## Language

This unit focuses on one use of the Present Perfect (i.e. to talk about past experience which has present importance – it doesn't matter when exactly the experience happened). This contrasts with the Past Simple tense (see Review Unit 3) which is used to talk about specific, completed events in the past which are psychologically distanced by the speaker from now.

Note that the other (related) use of the Present Perfect, to talk about 'unfinished time' with *since* and *for*, is practised in Unit 13.

## Common problems
### Present Perfect

The Present Perfect is extremely difficult for most students for the following reasons:

**1** In English, the Present Perfect indicates how the speaker sees the past in relation to the present – it doesn't indicate the past itself (i.e. strictly speaking it is not a tense like the Past Simple but a perfective 'aspect'). In some ways, because of its strong links with the present, it could be seen as more of a present verb form. In some other languages, however, (e.g. Arabic, Swedish and all European languages except Portuguese) the Present Perfect can be used to talk about definite past time: *\*I have been there yesterday.*

**2** In some languages (e.g. Farsi) the Present Perfect equivalent is formed with the verb *be*.

**3** Not all past participles are regular (see SB page 148). In some non-European languages there is no mother tongue equivalent of a past participle.

**4** Definite time expressions (e.g. *yesterday*) only go with the Past Simple. Indefinite time expressions (e.g. *yet*) only go with the Present Perfect. Notice in American English you can say: *'Did you see that film yet?' 'Yes, I already saw it.'*

**5** Some SS might find the word order is difficult with pronouns (*I have never met him.*) and time expressions (compare *Have you seen him **yet**?* with *I've **already** seen him.* etc.).

**6** Pronunciation: consonant clusters *haven't/ hasn't*; the contracted auxiliary *he's* (/z/) *asked* versus *he's* (/s/) *seen*; confusion between *he's* and *his*; *she is* and *she has* both contract to *she's*.

## Question tags

**1** In virtually all other languages the tag is a fixed form (French: *n'est-ce pas?*).

**2** In some languages there are two fixed form tags, one for confirmation or correction, the other to invite agreement. In others the tag is used only to invite agreement. In English, intonation is crucial to the message (i.e. rising = wanting information; falling = expecting agreement).

**3** Auxiliaries are a problem, particularly the positive → negative / negative → positive changes (see the *Language reference*, Section 2) and the inclusion of *do/does/did* when there is no auxiliary.

## Spelling

In most languages spelling and pronunciation are more closely related than in English.

# READING 1

## Before reading

● **Exercise 1** Possible subjects: the weather; food; customs; clothes; holiday resorts; the people. This is a more productive exercise in a multinational class.

## Reading

Ask SS to look at the photograph and make guesses about the nationality and character of Richard Shortway. Before they read for the first time (in order to answer the gist questions in Exercise 1), tell them not to worry about unfamiliar words at this stage.

● **Exercise 2** Ask SS to read a second time. PW/ GW: compare answers. You might ask them whether this extract confirms their image of Britain (in relation to class, the weather, the services, the countryside). SS will need to understand Richard Shortway's character before speculating on what his view of their country would be, e.g. he is a bit of a cynic and a social snob; efficient services are very important to him, etc.

● **Exercise 3** Use the phrase **wonderful** *estate agents* (paragraph 4) to introduce 'irony' (i.e. he says the opposite of what he means to show his annoyance).

● **Exercises 5 and 6** These lead SS into the language focus of the unit (indefinite time versus definite time) and you might want to go on to the GRAMMAR REVIEW from here. Make sure SS try to work out the 'answers' before looking them up. (Possibly hold these exercises and come back to them later when working on the Present Perfect.)

READING 1 and READING 2 could be done as a 'jigsaw' activity (i.e. one group of SS could work on READING 1, another on READING 2 – they then compare the attitudes of Richard and Chantal towards living in England). Possibly get SS to talk about some of the similarities and differences between their country and Britain (i.e. the Britain described in the texts).

# VOCABULARY

## Deducing meaning

● **Exercise 1** Further practice of the skill practised in Review Units 2 and 3.

● **Exercise 2** Introduction to phrasal verbs (see also Units 10 and 15). Get SS to check their answers in the dictionary looking up under the verb (*turn, cut, put*). Tell them to choose the correct definition for the context.

● **Exercise 3** Possibly emphasise that American English and British English are very similar (see *Practical English Usage* – details in *Bibliography*). There is a further vocabulary exercise in the WB.

# READING 2

READING 2 could come before or after any grammar work is done on the Present Perfect. Notice the use of the Present Perfect (e.g. in the second paragraph: *Things **have changed**.*) and *used to* in the penultimate paragraph: *'I **used to** use it.'* (practised in Review Unit 3).

Get SS to predict Chantal Cüer's attitude towards England (from e.g. her picture, the fact that she is French).

You might need to tell SS what *pubs* are. However, get them to work out from the context: *quaint, filthy, gentlemanly attitudes, slam, spend a bomb on, concept.*

# GRAMMAR REVIEW

## Past experiences and events

The assumption is that SS have had exposure to the Present Perfect but have both fluency and accuracy problems with it. The focus then is on contrast with the Past Simple (practised in Review Unit 3) and practice.

● **Exercise 1** Controlled (but personalised). Aims to give practice of Present Perfect (indefinite time) versus Past Simple (definite time). Further exercise in the WB.

● **Exercise 2** Freer.

● **Exercise 3** A personalised exercise. Could be done instead of Exercises 1 and 2 if your SS have a good grasp of the Present Perfect.

## Time expressions

See *Longman English Grammar* (see *Bibliography*) for help with the position of time expressions in the sentence (sections 7.22 and 7.23) and *already* versus *yet* (section 7.28).

## Question tags

Possibly first revise reply questions (e.g. *Do you?*) and short answers (e.g. *No, I don't.*) from Review Unit 1.

There is a more difficult exercise in the WB.

# PRONUNCIATION

## Intonation in question tags

It is easier for SS to recognise the intonation than produce it, so focus a lot on the practice section and the 'certain' tags, which are more common (though you could argue recognition is more important). Possibly encourage SS to exaggerate.

## Contracted forms

Focuses on linkage in connected speech of Present Perfect, a difficult area both for recognition and production (e.g. in *Where's she ...* the contracted *'s* is almost lost). Show SS that *she is* and *she has* both contract to *she's*.

# LEARNING FOCUS

## Keeping a grammar book

Personalised grammars encourage SS to take responsibility for grammar and to get interested in it. Keep the process up throughout the course and give SS time to make notes and compare with each other. Possibly spend some time on 'file management' in general at this stage (i.e. comparing ways of planning, organising, filing and storing all written records, including homework). Perhaps encourage SS to show each other their grammars and compare with published grammars.

Encourage SS to become aware of their grammar problems (in relation to their mother tongue?; as revealed in written work?) and to focus on these in their grammar records and WB exercises.

## Ways of learning English

● **Exercises 1–4** Try to get SS to concentrate on what Dany is saying rather than how correct her English is. PW. Aim to get SS to compare their experiences or views of language learning and be more aware of the learning process. By reflecting on such things as correction, how they learn vocabulary and how they improve their pronunciation they should be able to make their strategies more efficient. There is a useful follow-up *Listening* exercise in the WB on the pros and cons of informal and formal language learning (see also *Learning to Learn* – details in *Bibliography*).

● **Exercise 5** GW. Discussion to make SS and T co-partners in the learning process. Also provides useful information for T. Ts should try not to feel threatened when SS discuss their classes but use the information to plan future lessons. Could be seen as a follow-up to Exercises 1–5 or an introduction to *Learner diaries* below.

## Learner diaries

First, discuss why SS should keep diaries, what kind of things to record, the importance of writing (at the very least to reinforce the language studied), etc.

PW/GW exercise. Note that the corrections are only given as examples of the symbols. The texts have not been completely corrected.

Discuss correction in general and how you will correct SS' written work. (If you have your own system of symbols be consistent: put them up in your room and encourage other Ts in your school to use them.) These are some possible correction strategies for the teacher to use with writing tasks.

– Use symbols to identify all the mistakes, getting SS to correct themselves or others before they re-write.
– Focus on one area (e.g. spelling) with each piece of written work.
– Get SS to suggest improvements in each others' work by using the symbols themselves.

Possibly ask SS the pros and cons of each method and which they prefer. SS should be made aware that most initial attempts at written work will be seen as a draft.

Encourage SS to keep diaries of their own. Discuss possible formats, the sort of things that could be included and their value (e.g. they help us become aware of development and problems). Since diaries are personal, don't *insist* SS show them to you, but from time to time encourage them to read back over their experiences and discuss with each other.

# WRITING

## Spelling

PW/GW. Make sure these self-correction techniques are employed throughout the course.

# Tapescripts

## RECORDING 1

a) You know Stephen, don't you?
b) They'll check the flight, won't they?
c) She took the dog for a walk, didn't she?
d) You've been here already, haven't you?
e) We don't need to book, do we?
f) She can swim, can't she?
g) You couldn't lend me some money, could you?

## RECORDING 2

1 Where's she been?
2 He's just come back from abroad.
3 She's already finished it.
4 He's had enough to drink, I think.
5 He says he's seen a ghost.

## RECORDING 3

Well, vocabulary for me is the most important thing. To be fluently, to be fluent you need vocabulary. I am always listen to music or watching TV or watching, listen to the radio, and then when I hear some words I keep them in my mind, and then one day after, or two, I still remember this word – I can't remember from where, but I still have it in my mind, then I start looking in the vocab-, in the dictionary or something like this. It's not just studying the vocabulary that the teacher give me in the class that I learn it. I learn it from, as I told you, from listen to music and television. Then to improve your English the most important thing is having new vocabulary because at the beginning you use always the same verbs and the same words.

I think if you are speaking with somebody – a friend or whatever, it's really important to be all the time trying to improve your English, not just to be fluent. I am always paying attention in my pronunciation. If I am talking to somebody, when I finish it I, I start thinking about what I said and trying to correct myself, even if I had made mistakes. I think it's very important to, to try to use correct words, correct verbs and pronunciation.

I really like to be corrected all the time, not just when I write but when I am speaking. If I am with someone chatting, I like when people corrected me.

# Key

## READING 1

### Reading

**1**

a) American.

b) His impression is generally good, though he has reservations.

**2**

a) He loves the people and the social atmosphere (at least of the 'high society').

b) The public services are inefficient (gas board, telephones); estate agents and the system of buying and selling houses are bad.

c) The weather is bad. (Summer only seemed to last a week last year!)

d) He loves both the big city (London) and the countryside (Cotswolds and Devon).

e) The cost of living is very high. London is just as expensive as New York.

**3**

He doesn't like them. When he says they are *wonderful* he is being ironic. He actually means he has a very low opinion of them.

**4**

He talks a lot about mixing with royalty. We assume that when he says he loves the people and the ambience he is talking about 'high society'.

**5**

He says *I've met* because he is talking about something he has experienced. He is not referring to when it happened. He says he *had* a long talk with Prince Charles because he is referring to a specific occasion (a particular polo match).

**6**

a) He's been invited to everything. He's been to shooting parties, polo, Wimbledon and Royal Ascot; he's tried to deal with British Gas and British Telecom; he's tried to call America by phone; he's dealt with estate agents and been gazumped; he's played a little tennis but not much; he's been to the Cotswolds and to Devon.

b) He went to the Cotswolds and to Devon last summer. (Past Simple)

## VOCABULARY

### Deducing meaning

**1**

a) The company that runs the telephone system in Britain.

b) People whose business it is to buy and sell houses.

c) Someone refused to sell a house to him (even though he had agreed to buy it) and sold it instead to someone else who offered more money.

**2**

a) stop (ii)   b) disconnect (i)   c) pay (i)

**3**

a) phone   b) engaged tone   c) man

## READING 2

**1**

When she first came to England she really liked it: the houses, the countryside, the pubs, London. Now her opinions have changed: London is filthy; the people are rude; there are not many nice places where you can meet people; public transport is dangerous (particularly for women); families are not very closely knit (unlike in France).

## GRAMMAR REVIEW

### Time expressions

a) already/just

b) recently

c) recently / in November

d) yet

e) before

f) already

g) in November / recently / two seconds ago

h) always

### Question tags

b) won't they?   c) didn't she?   d) haven't you?

e) do we?   f) can't she?   g) could you?

## PRONUNCIATION

### Intonation in question tags

Certain: a), b), e)   Uncertain: c), d), f), g)

### Contracted forms

1 Where's she been? (*4 words*)

2 He's just come back from abroad. (*7 words*)

3 She's already finished it. (*5 words*)

4 He's had enough to drink, I think. (*8 words*)

5 He says he's seen a ghost. (*7 words*)

## LEARNING FOCUS

### Ways of learning English

**1**

a)  i) Disagree. (*Vocabulary for me is the most important thing*)

ii) Agree. (*I learn it from … listen to music and television*)

iii) Disagree. (*I learn it from … listen to music and television*)

iv) Disagree. (*I start thinking about what I said and trying to correct myself*)

v) Agree. (*I really like to be corrected all the time*)

### Learner diaries

b) *t* – tense; *v* – vocabulary; *L* – word missing; *g* – grammar; *sp* – spelling; *p* – punctuation

## WRITING

### Spelling

**1**

a) receipt   b) miserable   c) smiling   d) scissors

e) examination   f) happier

**2**

b) imagining (not *imagineing*); experience (not *expereince*); depressed (not *depresed*); necessary (not *neccesary*); practised (not *practiced*)

# A bit windy

## Language

The language focus of this unit is on ways of
talking about the future using *will* and *going to*. SS
will already have been exposed to these
constructions and will probably know how to form
them – the main problem is when to use them.
Unlike many other languages English does not
have a 'future tense' as such, simply different ways
of talking about the future, depending on how the
speaker sees the future event at the moment of
speaking. The speaker could be making a
prediction or stating an intention based on
(evidence of) a process that has already begun
(using *going to*) or making a personal decision or
spontaneous prediction in reaction to a present
event (*will*). Future forms are an area of great
difficulty for learners of English.

The other common way of talking about the
future – using the Present Continuous – is
introduced in Unit 10, although SS will probably
already have been exposed to it. There is also
further revision in Unit 10 of *will* and the Future
Passive. Modals such as *may* and *might* to talk
about the future are introduced in Unit 9. The
Future Continuous and Future Perfect are
introduced in *Upper Intermediate Matters*.

## Common problems

In many other languages the present tense is used
to talk about the future when the sense is clear
from the context.

### Will

**1**  SS often use this inappropriately (instead of
*going to* or the Present Continuous) to talk about
planned decisions for the future (*\*Tomorrow I will
visit my friend.*).

**2**  Spontaneous intentions or decisions which
happen in reaction to a present state or event and
which can express promises, threats, etc.
depending on context, are often expressed by the
present tense in many languages (*\*I phone you
later.*).

**3** SS need to be encouraged to use the contracted form (*'ll*) whenever possible. They also frequently confuse the pronunciation of *won't* (/wəʊnt/) and *want* (/wɒnt/) and also *will* (/wɪl/) and *we'll* (/wɪəl/).

**4** SS often confuse *shall* and *will* because they have been taught that they should use *shall* with *I* and *we*. In fact, in native speaker connected speech the contracted form (*'ll*) is most often used. It is important that the use of *shall* for suggestions and offers is made clear. There is an exercise on this in the WB.

### Going to

**1** In some languages (e.g. German, Greek) there is no equivalent to *going to*.

**2** Spanish speakers often over-use *going to*.

**3** The pronunciation is often weakened so that *to* (/tuː/) becomes *to* (/t ə/). SS will probably be familiar with *gonna* (/ɡʌnə/), often used in pop songs.

**4** *Going to go* is usually shortened to *going to* (*I am going to the theatre tomorrow.*).

# LISTENING

## Before listening

● **Exercise 1** This should elicit vocabulary such as *gales, floods,* and *hurricanes*.

● **Exercise 2** Useful revision of the Present Perfect and the contrast with the Past Simple (e.g. *A snowstorm has hit Britain. This morning much of Britain was covered in snow.*). Use the photos to generate as much weather vocabulary as you can (this will be useful later in the unit) and encourage SS to add any expressions they know. You might want to comment on the fact that even not very extreme weather conditions (e.g. as in the photo of the snow) can cause havoc in Britain!

● **Exercise 3, c)** Give examples (e.g. the tendency for many warmer countries to open their shops/offices, etc. earlier and keep them open until very late, but close at lunchtime for a rest, compared to the hours kept by Britain and other northern European countries).

## Listening

● **Exercises 1 and 2** Note that Recordings 1 and 2 follow on from each other. The first one is Michael Fish, the British TV weather forecaster, who became famous for his prediction, just before the hurricanes which took place in Britain in November 1989. Play the first recording for gist. Then ask SS to listen to the second recording, which took place the following day, and answer Exercise 2 a). They may be able to try and complete the gapped summary before listening a second time to check their answers. Point out the use of *will* in the recording to show the speaker's certainty.

● **Exercises 3 and 4** The listening texts exemplify the use of the Present Perfect to introduce recent events which are important now, and the Past Simple when giving further detailed information. They provide a model for the news broadcast SS are asked to prepare later in the unit. If SS find this difficult they might want to read the tapescript (full edition of the SB only) while they listen.

Note the use of the passive construction with the Present Perfect and Past Simple in the reports, e.g. *Power supplies **have been disrupted** and large sections of the rail network **were left** out of action.* You may want to do a little revision or presentation of the Present Perfect / Past Simple Passive (*'What have been torn off? How many people were killed?'*) at this stage before Unit 19, where the passive is focused on in greater detail.

# VOCABULARY 1

## Weather

● **Exercises 1–4** Encourage SS to use dictionaries for these exercises. This vocabulary links to the LISTENING AND SPEAKING activities which come later in the unit. Indicate that Exercise 1 is a collocation exercise (more work on collocation is done in Unit 19). You may want to suggest that SS keep a 'weather' section in their vocabulary notebooks. There is more practice of weather vocabulary in the WB.

● **Exercises 5 and 6** These provide revision of the Present Continuous as well as vocabulary studied in the unit. Possibly extend to a comparison of the weather in the SS' own country.

# LANGUAGE POINT 1

## Predictions and decisions

● **Exercise 1**   The difference in use between *will* and *going to* is difficult for SS to grasp. Summarise the different uses of both with the SS, referring them to the *Language reference*, and possibly follow up the exercise with a personalised example. For example, contrast a planned decision (*'He's going to stay at this school for two months.'*) with a spontaneous one (*'I'll just close the window. I'm cold.'*) and a personal prediction based on certainty (*'It'll get warmer in May.'*) with one based on evidence of the situation (*'We're not going to finish this unit today – we've only got twenty minutes left!'*).

Use situations relevant to your own SS where possible.

● **Exercise 1**   In eliciting the answers point out and demonstrate the contracted form of *will* and the weak form of *to* in *going to*. Possibly do a quick drill around the class to practise the form and pronunciation of these forms. Also, draw SS' attention to the pronunciation of *won't* /wəʊnt/ (a diphthong) and the possible confusion with *want* (/wɒnt/) (no diphthong).

# PRACTICE

● **Exercise 1**   PW/GW. Report back each others' plans to the class. Monitor pronunciation here.

● **Exercise 2**   Should be done individually. Read it through first with SS to check they know the vocabulary.

● **Exercise 3**   Other examples could be:
Opinions: *I'm positive*; *I bet*; *I'm convinced*; *In my view*.
Time expressions: *by the end of the century*; *in my lifetime*; *in the future*.

● **Exercise 4**   Could be extended to groups making their own predictions and other groups agreeing or disagreeing (note the language of agreeing/disagreeing has been practised in Review Unit 3). Headings could be elicited and put on the board, e.g. *Medicine*; *Health*; *Science*; *Food*; *Relationships*.

● **Exercises 5 and 6**   PW. Discuss the reasons why SS chose *will* or *going to* in order to reinforce their understanding of the differences in use. There is another exercise in the WB.

# LANGUAGE POINT 2

## Verbs and prepositions

There is more work on this in the WB. Remind SS to make a note of the preposition which follows a verb in their vocabulary books, and perhaps show them how to check in the dictionary prepositions which follow verbs.

# LISTENING AND SPEAKING

● **Exercises 1–3**   Intended to be a lighthearted introduction to the British habit of discussing the weather, and an opportunity to use some of the more useful vocabulary actively. Remind SS of the adjectives of likes and dislikes from Review Unit 1 (*awful*, *wonderful*, etc.).

# READING AND SPEAKING

## A news broadcast

● **Exercise 1**   Encourage SS to read the article quickly to answer the questions. Give them a time limit, and write the answers on the board.

● **Exercise 2**   If necessary, play a snippet of the recording again. It might be an idea to get all the As, Bs and Cs to work together first and plan what they are going to say, before splitting them up into their groups. You could also include interviews with the two old men, George Kidd and Willie Ollington, if you wished.

The interviews could be acted out and recorded or videoed. Ask SS to monitor their use of Past Simple and Past Continuous during the playback.

## VOCABULARY 2

### Telephoning

● **Exercise 1** The vocabulary in this exercise might be useful for CREATIVE WRITING.

● **Exercises 2 and 3** Monitor the SS' intonation when they are practising the dialogue in pairs. Could develop into a discussion of ways of answering the phone (saying the number, etc.) in different countries, and also the use of cardphones and credit cards. There is an exercise in the WB on words such as *receiver, dial*, etc.

A suggested extra practice activity could involve: a) making a call (what do you say?); and b) answering a call (in the home / in the office).

## CREATIVE WRITING

● **Exercise 1** PW/GW. A discussion activity, making use of the weather vocabulary introduced earlier as well as both past and future forms. In discussion encourage SS to use the language of opinion and agreeing/disagreeing used in this and previous units (e.g. Review Unit 3).

● **Exercise 2** PW? Individual?

● **Exercise 5** GW or in front of the class? Possibly record or video the dialogues – should give useful feedback as to how accurately SS are using past and future forms.

# Tapescripts

### RECORDING 1

Earlier on today, apparently, a woman rang the BBC and said she heard that there was a hurricane on the way. Well, if you're watching, don't worry, there isn't. But, having said that, actually the weather will become very windy, but most of the strong winds incidentally will be down over Spain and across into France.

### RECORDING 2

The great cleaning-up operation is now underway in the wake of the hurricane-force winds which battered much of southern England in the small hours. At least thirteen people are known to have died and many were injured, hit by falling trees and masonry toppled in the gales. Power supplies have been disrupted and large sections of the rail network were left out of action. Our reporters have been assessing the scale of the chaos and the damage. We begin with the latest from the south coast.

### RECORDING 3

This is David Smeeton in Southampton. In the southern region it's been a day of assessing the damage to hundreds of roofs, many of them torn completely off, while some homes are partially collapsed. Overnight scores of people were looked after in emergency centres …

And finally this is Andrew Roberts with a look at how the storms have affected the capital. Two people were killed as winds of 94 miles an hour – the highest ever recorded – gusted across London. In Croydon a motorist died when his car was crushed by a falling tree.

### RECORDING 4

[A collection of 'weather sounds': pouring rain; a very violent wind; the sound of crunching snow; a crash of thunder.]

### RECORDING 5

A: What do you think of this weather we're having, then?
B: Bit too hot for my liking. Can't breathe, it's so close. Brings on my cough something terrible. Give me a bit of cold any day!
A: I don't know what's happening to our climate.
B: What do you mean?
A: Hot one day, snowing the next. It was different in our day.
B: Can't be healthy, all this sun.
A: You're right. And it dries up the garden like nobody's business …

# Key

## LISTENING

### Before listening

**1**
a) 2  b) 1  c) 4  d) 3

**2**
1  It has been snowing.
2  There has been flooding along the coast.
3  There has been a bad drought. (There hasn't been any rain for a long time.)
4  There has been a hurricane.

### Listening

**1**
Summary c).

**2**
a)  For making a wrong prediction in the weather forecast.
b)  1  southern
    2  thirteen
    3  injured
    4  trees
    5  gales
    6  supplies
    7  rail
    8  chaos
    9  damage
    10  latest

**3**
a)  This is … in ….
b)  Present Perfect.
c)  Past Simple.

**4**
a)  Hundreds of roofs.
b)  Some homes.
c)  Scores of people were looked after.
d)  Two.
e)  Ninety-four miles an hour.
f)  A tree crushed his car while he was in it.

## VOCABULARY 1

### Weather

**1**
heavy rain; thick fog/cloud; strong wind; dense fog/cloud

**2**
a) showers  b) pouring  c) dull, overcast  d) drizzling

**3**
hurricane, gale, strong wind, breeze

**4**
b) boiling  d) heavy and close  c) mild  a) chilly
e) freezing

**6**
1  It's raining heavily.
2  It's very windy.
3  It's been snowing.
4  There's a thunderstorm.

## LANGUAGE POINT 1

### Predictions and decisions

**1**
a) 3  b) 4  c) 1  d) 2

## PRACTICE

**5**
a)  I'll go
b)  He's going to
c)  it'll be
d)  she'll love
e)  I'm going to finish; I'll probably watch
f)  I'll phone
g)  you're going to order; I'll have

**6**
a)  'I'm going to paint the bathroom white (etc.) …'
b)  'I'm going to buy them …'
c)  'Look, it's going to rain.'
d)  'Don't worry. I'm sure you'll pass.'
e)  'Be careful or you'll hurt yourself.'

## LANGUAGE POINT 2

### Verbs and prepositions

**1**
a) for  b) with  c) on  d) about  e) about  f) in
g) on  h) in  i) of/about  j) for

## LISTENING AND SPEAKING

**1**
See tapescript for Recording 5.

## READING AND SPEAKING

### A news broadcast

**1**
a)  Two delivery men: Mr Philip Shaw and a colleague (no name given). Two men in car: Mr George Kidd and Mr William Ollington.
b)  Mr Kidd and Mr Ollington were rescued by two delivery men, Mr Shaw and his colleague, when a tree crashed down on the roof of Mr Kidd's car during a gale last Thursday. The two delivery men had to break the windscreen of the car in order to pull the trapped men out. It was the second time in two years that a car belonging to Mr Kidd had been crushed by a tree. Both times Mr Kidd had been driving a yellow car.
c)  It was very windy.

## VOCABULARY 2

### Telephoning

**1**
A: e), b), g), d), c), h), a), f)
B: c), b), d), a), f), e)

# Are you 'green'?

## Students' Book

**General theme:** the natural world.
**Unit topic:** the environment.

**READING:** magazine article on the 'ungreen' Moore family.
**LISTENING AND SPEAKING:** interview with Mrs Moore; questionnaire: *How 'green' are you?*

**LANGUAGE POINT 1:** defining relative clauses.
**LANGUAGE POINT 2:** clauses of purpose.

**PRONUNCIATION:** syllable stress: weak syllables – the *schwa* (/ə /).
**VOCABULARY:** adjectives with *-ed* and *-ing*; adjectives from nouns and verbs (suffixes: *-y*, *-ous*, *-ic*, *-ful*, *-able*, *-al*, *-ive*).
**WRITING:** semi-formal letters; clauses of result and reason.

## Workbook

**LISTENING:** children talking about the environment.
**GRAMMAR:** defining relative clauses; clauses of result and reason; clauses of purpose.
**VOCABULARY:** town and country; adjectives with *-ing* or *-ed*.
**WRITING:** semi-formal and personal writing styles; dictation.

## Language

This unit focuses on sentence structure, in particular defining relative clauses (sometimes known as 'identifying' or 'restrictive' clauses); clauses of purpose and clauses of result and reason.

## Common problems
### Defining relative clauses

Defining relative clauses are much more common in spoken English than non-defining relative clauses (see *Upper Intermediate Matters* for non-defining relative clauses). SS who have learnt English in a formal teaching situation usually have some familiarity with them but have problems using them naturally and correctly, partly because in informal English short, economical forms are preferred (e.g. *the girl in the red dress / the girl wearing the red dress* rather than *the girl who is wearing the red dress*). In addition SS have problems with when the relative pronoun can be left out (see the *Language reference*) and also with where to place a preposition (in conversational English it can often come at the end of a relative clause: *That's the woman I used to work with.*).

Also:

**1**   In some languages (e.g. Farsi and Swiss German) there is one relative pronoun for both things and people (*\*A boy which …*).

**2**   In English, relative clauses are post-modifiers (they come after the noun). In Turkish, for example, they come before the noun.

**3**   For some speakers (e.g. German and Dutch) the word *what* is used for *which* (*\*The thing what …*) and most West Europeans will try to say *\*Don't believe all what he says.*

**4**   In some languages (e.g. Greek and Arabic) the object of the verb must be included in the clause (*\*This is the car which I bought it yesterday.*).

### Clauses of purpose

Common mistakes:

*We left early for (to) get there on time.* (especially Spanish speakers)

*We left early to got there on time.* (e.g. Greek speakers)

### Clauses of result and reason

A common mistake (e.g. for Chinese speakers) is to duplicate connecting words: *Because they have a hot climate, so it is essential ...*

### Pronunciation: the *schwa*

SS often give unstressed vowels their stressed value (e.g. /ðiː/ for /ðə/ *the*).

# READING

## Before reading

● **Exercise 1**   Other environmental problems: destruction of wild life; air pollution from car fumes causing bad health, etc.

● **Exercise 2**   The Green Party aims to get political power and protect the environment. Ask if there is a Green Party in the SS' own country/ countries.

## Reading

In multinational classes, be careful: not all countries have the same level of sympathy for and awareness of environmental issues and scientific jargon (e.g. 'CFCs').

Remember your main focus is on linguistic issues so try not to get too doom-laden or evangelical; also, as can be seen from the LISTENING section, it is not easy to be 'green'.

Don't milk the subject dry too soon – you'll need to sustain interest into the next section.

● **Exercise 1**   Tricky text for vocabulary but most of the words can be deduced from context or with the help of the pictures. Use as a skimming/ scanning exercise and discourage the use of dictionaries at this stage.

● **Exercise 2**   Get SS to discuss the meanings.

● **Exercise 3**   Text is good for subordinate clauses (e.g. relative clauses). This exercise (PW/ GW) is a good opportunity to build up awareness of 'reference', so a good idea to do some

follow-up work in later units (e.g. by asking what this pronoun/determiner refers to).

Encourage dictionary work to check guesses made.

● **Exercise 4**   Ask how environmental attitudes are similar/different in SS' own country/countries; personalise the subject (e.g. *'What things worry you?'*).

# LISTENING AND SPEAKING

These activities help balance the argument against the Moores and encourage debate. (It could actually be used as a stimulus for a full-scale debate.)

● **Exercise 2**   Young SS may not have direct experience of buying the things referred to, so ask them to think of their parents. Ask SS to check in the dictionary for the meaning and pronunciation of unknown words.

After using the LISTENING exercise in the WB, you could get SS to devise their own questionnaire (or use or adapt this one) and interview children about environmental issues (particularly useful in Britain). They could then report back or write a report.

# LANGUAGE POINT 1

## Defining relative clauses

Discourage SS from looking at the *Language reference* until they have tried Exercise 1. Possibly point out that instead of *where* you can use *that/ which* + preposition (*at/in*).

# PRACTICE

● **Exercise 1**   Personalised fluency exercise.

● **Exercise 2**   Accuracy exercise. PW/GW: check answers? Further practice in the WB if needed. Relative clauses lend themselves well to quizzes: *What's the name of the person who ... ?*

## LANGUAGE POINT 2

### Clauses of purpose

Encourage SS to use both constructions with each sentence. Discourage attempts at this stage to use other ways of expressing purpose (e.g. prepositional phrases: *for* + *-ing*; formal constructions: *in order to/that*, *so as to*, etc.). You might want to introduce the negative (*not to*; *so that ... not*) but it can be avoided. Possibly get SS to think of their own examples.

## PRONUNCIATION

● **Exercise 2**   You could ask SS to predict the syllables which contain schwas and check their answers by listening. Possibly get SS to use the phonemic chart (SB page 149) to transcribe the words and check answers in the dictionary. A good place to do more work on sounds.

In future, when SS come across a new word, get them not only to identify word stress but also any weakened sounds.

## VOCABULARY

### Adjectives

● **Exercise 1**   Focuses on 'reaction' adjectives (good revision of *-ed* endings).

● **Exercise 2**   Shows how they can change meaning by adding *-ing*.

● **Exercise 3**   Extends into other suffixes.

Personalise the difference between *-ed* and *-ing*: *'Are you bored in class or boring? Are you interesting or interested?'* Make sure SS note down the prepositions that go with them. Common problem: confusion of *bored* and *annoyed*.

Get SS to add columns of words with the same suffix to their vocabulary books.

## WRITING

### Semi-formal letters

The English conventions for semi-formal letter writing are almost certainly different from those SS are used to and will need practice. Knowing the right formulas to use and being accurate is very important in this kind of writing. (See, by contrast, the personal letter in Unit 7.)

● **Exercises 1–3**   (PW/GW?) Link the relationship between addressor and addressee and the purpose of writing with the layout, format and style of letter. Exercise 4 focuses on the kind of phrases found in semi-formal letters.

● **Exercise 1**   You might want to start with some work on the content of the letter before going on to Exercise 2 (e.g. by asking SS what information they have learnt from the letter, what they agree/ disagree with, etc.).

● **Exercise 2**   The results can be a 'template' for SS when writing their own semi-formal letters.

● **Exercise 3**   Make sure SS realise that contractions are not normally used in this kind of writing. In general, a semi-formal style is tightly-organised, factual and linked to conventional modes of address.

● **Exercise 4**   Can be extended by asking SS to rewrite some phrases in the letter to make them less formal: e.g. *I am writing to express my concern*; *so it is essential that we ...*; *one in every four products obtained ...*

● **Exercise 5**   Extends out of the text into a grammatical area (clauses of result and reason) common in writing. Make sure you read the *Language reference* if you are uncertain which linkers normally start a new sentence. (Note there are other exercises with linkers in Review Unit 3 and Units 8 and 17.)

Don't let these exercises become heavy. Make sure there is a lot of discussion. Compare conventions and style with what SS are used to in their own country. If there is too much work in this section for the time available, cut out either Exercise 4 or 5 or set them for homework.

● **Exercise 6**   Make sure SS spend sufficient time planning the letter – it'll make their task easier later. Get them to do a first draft, then try and improve each others' before writing it up. Alternatively, the whole letter could be composed in groups. If you mark it don't forget to use a marking scheme (see Review Unit 4). An alternative exercise might be to get SS to write a real letter to a real person about something they feel strongly about.

# Tapescripts

## RECORDING 1

INTERVIEWER: This week's *Going green* interview comes from the home of Mrs Julia Moore. Mrs Moore, good morning.

MRS MOORE: Morning.

INTERVIEWER: Mrs Moore, an article was written about you and your family recently called, 'Are these people criminals?' Do you feel it's just and fair for people to say that in your life-style you commit crimes against the environment?

MRS MOORE: Well, no, I don't feel it's fair, because actually we do care about the environment, but the reality is I'm a working mum with two small children and I simply do not have the time to put all the principles that you could put into action in action. For example, if we take shopping to start with, you know, I do try to buy environmentally-friendly products if they are available, but quite often they are not on offer, so for example, you can't buy ozone-friendly flyspray. And for example with things like meat, me and my husband, Derek, avoid eating too much meat, but the children like sausages and they get them outside the home and so I do buy meat from time to time. With fruit, well, I try to buy loose unpackaged fruit but sometimes you just run out of time and that's what it's all about, you know: I just want to go into the shops, do my shopping once a week and then leave.

And then moving on to getting rid of the rubbish afterwards and the whole recycling issue. You know, OK, there are bottle banks around but they are difficult to find. They are often full. I don't like having glass bottles at home because if they get broken then they are obviously dangerous. And the same with newspapers. You end up with stacks and stacks of newspapers. If there was someone to take them away that would be fine, and I actually do believe it's the Government's responsibility. If dustbinmen took away sorted rubbish that would be fine, but as they don't, you know we just don't have the time and the energy to, to dispose of all this rubbish ourselves.

And then finally the whole sort of thing about transport. Well, we use lead-free petrol, but travelling on public transport with two small children really isn't an option, it's just not practical: it's dirty, it's unreliable, and it's expensive. I mean you can wait hours for buses and trains and they don't turn up.

You know if I try to put everything, all my principles, into action, can you imagine? I'd be hauling the children round on buses with bags full of heavy, broken glass bottles – I really wouldn't have time to do anything else with my life.

## RECORDING 2

a) machine   b) animals   c) banana   d) environment
e) chemicals   f) suggestion   g) tropical   h) Parliament

## RECORDING 3

a) I don't like the colour.
b) Robert's a very good actor.
c) The pollution here is dreadful.
d) That armchair's very comfortable.
e) What an intelligent elephant!

# Key

## READING

### Reading

**1**

1 f  2 j  3 e  4 a  5 b  6 d  7 h  8 c  9 g  10 i

**2**

a) A gas screen above the earth's surface that helps protect us from the harmful rays of the sun.
b) Rain containing harmful quantities of acid as a result of industrial pollution.
c) A farm with lines of small boxes in which hens are kept and specially treated so that they lay eggs frequently.
d) The gradual warming of the earth's atmosphere because heat cannot escape through its upper layers.
e) To treat something which has already been used (paper, bottles, etc.) so that it can be used again.

**3**

a) Julia Moore's spray
b) the ozone layer
c) chlorofluorocarbons (CFCs)
d) the wasting of power by cooking pots boiling over
e) organic fruit and vegetables
f) carbon dioxide
g) plastic shopping bags
h) washing powders and cleaners

**4**

Fly spray; CFCs; washing power; burning oil and coal; acid rain; pesticides; fertilisers; battery farms; cutting down rain forests (using hardwood; eating meat); carbon dioxide (the 'greenhouse effect'); plastic bags; throwing out rubbish instead of recycling it; insecticides.

## LISTENING AND SPEAKING

**1**

*Shopping*: environmentally-friendly products often not available.
*Food*: children like sausages; no time to buy loose, unpackaged fruit.
*Recycling*: bottle banks difficult to find – often full; broken bottles at home dangerous; too much paper; no time to sort paper; no-one to take them away.
*Transport*: public transport with children not practical – dirty, unreliable, expensive; long waits – often don't turn up.

## LANGUAGE POINT 1

### Defining relative clauses

**1**

a) whose   b) who, that   c) that, which   d) where

**2**

The relative pronoun can be left out in a), b) and e).

## PRACTICE

**2**

a) I saw a film yesterday *that/which* really terrified me.
b) That was my mother (*who*) you met last week.
c) Let's go to that nice restaurant *where* we ate on my birthday (*that/which* we ate *in* on my birthday).
d) Margaret's an energetic person *who/that* hardly ever sleeps.
e) I have contact lenses (*that/which*) you can wear all the time.
f) She's the woman *whose* car we bought.
g) Have you worn those new shoes (*that/which*) I bought you yet?
h) A microwave is a machine *that/which* cooks food.
i) John Lennon was a famous singer *who* was in a group called 'The Beatles'.
j) Look, that's the house *where* you were born (*that/which* you were born *in*).

## LANGUAGE POINT 2

### Clauses of purpose

Example answers:
a) To get wood for furniture. / So that the wood can be made into pulp for paper.
b) To kill insects which destroy their crops.
c) To get the ivory from their tusks, which is then sold and made into ornaments.
d) So that they get slim and live longer.
e) So that we can relax.

## PRONUNCIATION

**1**

a) ma'chine
b) 'animals
c) ba'nana
d) en'vironment
e) 'chemicals
f) su'ggestion
g) 'tropical
h) 'Parliament

**2**

a) I don't like the colour.
b) Robert's a very good actor.
c) The pollution here is dreadful.
d) That armchair's very comfortable.
e) What an intelligent elephant!

## VOCABULARY

### Adjectives

**1**

1 bored   2 interested   3 disappointed   4 amused
5 tired   6 annoyed

**2**

a) boring   b) amusing   c) interested   d) disappointed
e) tiring   f) annoyed

**3**

attractive, colourful, religious, sympathetic, romantic, criminal, dirty, hopeful, imaginative

# WRITING
## Semi-formal letters

**1**

Sarah Trebbit is writing to her MP, Mr Adam Crew. The letter aims to get the MP to persuade the Government to cancel Third World debts, so that countries are not forced to cut down their rain forests to earn money to repay those debts.

**2**

a) 7  b) 2  c) 9  d) 3  e) 10  f) 6  g) 1  h) 8
i) 11  j) 4  k) 5

**3**

a) ii) True
   iii) False
   iv) True
   v) True
b) Start: *Dear Sir/Madam*
   Close: *Yours faithfully,*

**4**

1 c)  2 e)  3 a)  4 f)  5 g)  6 b)  7 d)

**5**

a)  i) result; reason   ii) result; reason
b)  i) There are many droughts *because/as/since* …
       *Because/As/Since* the world's temperatures are
          rising, there …
       The world's temperatures are rising *so there* …
       The world's temperatures are rising. *Therefore / As
          a result / That's why* …
    ii) I didn't vote for the 'Green Party'
          *because/as/since* …
       *Because/As/Since* I didn't think the 'Green Party'
          could win, I …
       I didn't think the 'Green Party' could win *so* …
       I didn't think the 'Green Party' could win.
          *Therefore / As a result / That's why* I …

# Choosing a partner

## Students' Book

**General theme:** people and places.
**Unit topic:** relationships.

**VOCABULARY:** adjectives describing personality and appearance.
**LISTENING:** two couples talking about their partners.
**SPEAKING 1:** describing partners/students in the class.

**LANGUAGE POINT 1:** asking for descriptions (*is like / look like / like + -ing*).
**LANGUAGE POINT 2:** putting adjectives in the right order.
**LANGUAGE POINT 3:** possessive -*s* (*the cat's name*, etc.), including pronunciation.
**LANGUAGE POINT 4:** adverbs of manner (*politely*, etc.).
**LANGUAGE POINT 5:** adverbs of degree (*a bit*, *very*, etc.).

**READING:** two surveys on what men/women want in a partner.
**SPEAKING 2:** discussion on pros and cons of marriage / living alone, etc.
**WRITING:** writing a personal letter.

## Workbook

**READING:** extract from a popular, romantic novel.
**VOCABULARY:** adjectives and adverbs; relationships (*get married to*, etc.); parts of the body; expressions using parts of the body (*nosy*, etc.).
**GRAMMAR:** adjective word order; possessives.
**PRONUNCIATION:** sound and spelling: the *schwa* (/ə /).

## Language

This unit focuses on the language used to describe people, in particular adjectives and adverbs.

## Common problems

### What ... like / look like?

The question *What is ... like?* is given attention because it is very common in English and causes SS a lot of problems. The main reasons are:
– the equivalent question in many languages (e.g. Italian) would be translated literally *How is ... ?*
– the confusion between *What does he like?*, *What is he like?* and *What does he look like?* (See the *Language reference* for the differences.) A persistent error is *\*How was it like?*

In some cases it is possible to use *How is/was ... ?* as well as *What is/was ... like?* when we focus on personal reactions (e.g. **How was** the book? / **What was** the book **like**?), although this use has been avoided in this unit to reduce the possibility of confusion.

### Adjectives and adverbs

Adjectives and adverbs behave differently in many languages, and SS tend to overuse adjectives and avoid adverbs. These are some of the problems.

**1** In many languages (e.g. Swahili, Latin languages, Vietnamese) attributive adjectives come after the noun: *\*She is (a) woman young.*

**2** In English, 'action' verbs normally take adverbs. However, in some languages (e.g. Arabic) adjectives and adverbs are identical: *\*He speaks English very good.* In English, after verbs of perception (e.g. *seem, smell, look*) we normally use adjectives. However, in some languages (e.g. Japanese and Scandinavian languages), the reverse is true: *\*He looks smartly.*

**3** In some languages (e.g. Greek, Arabic and Latin languages) adjectives are inflected: *\*reds chairs.*

**4** In, for example, Japanese some 'adjectives'

behave like verbs: *That man tall*. In other languages they can function as nouns: *You poor! I feel sorry for you*.

**5**  Some adjectives end in *-ly* (*ugly*), but some *-ly* words can be both adjectives and adverbs (*monthly*) and some non *-ly* words can be both adjectives and adverbs (*fast*).

**6**  Word order is also a problem because in English we prefer a particular sequence when there is more than one adjective. However, the 'rules' are not fixed and a lot depends on the speaker's emphasis.

**7**  Other word order problems: *He speaks very well English*.

### Possessive -s

**1**  In many languages (e.g. the Latin languages) possessives are expressed with an *of*-phrase: *The career of Charles*.

**2**  With non-living things we say: *the leg of the table* (or *the table leg*) not *the table's leg*.

# VOCABULARY

Get SS to say which words in the boxes relate to which people. Possibly use *He/She seems/looks …* SS can ask each other the meaning of unknown words and/or check in a dictionary.

Possibly ask SS to describe one of the people in the pictures and other SS guess who it is.

# LISTENING

## Before listening

The *Listening* exercises link to the preceding VOCABULARY exercises. Make the guessing game fairly light (notice one of the people is the 'odd one out') and encourage free use of adjectival phrases so you can diagnose any accuracy problems. Can be followed up in the LANGUAGE POINTS and WB but use the *Listening* for SS to check their guesses first.

## Listening

- **Exercise 1**  Can be done as PW.

- **Exercise 2**  Make sure SS write notes under the names according to what their partners say about them (not what they themselves say). Ensure correct use of adjectives in notes (e.g. word order). Note useful adverbs of degree used in the recordings (*very, quite, incredibly, completely, extremely*), useful vocabulary such as *mature* and *bright*, and fillers such as *you know* and *well*. Mention that Françoise is French.

- **Exercise 5**  Links well to LANGUAGE POINTS 1 (*look like*) and 2 (adjective word order). Possibly use pictures of people to elicit vocabulary.

## SPEAKING 1

- **Exercise 1**  Student A and Student B can change over (reduce sentences from five to three?).

- **Exercise 2**  Can be done as GW or with a student at the front or in the middle of room. To sustain concentration keep to the limit on the number of questions.

# LANGUAGE POINT 1

## Asking for descriptions

Spend time sorting out use (refer to the *Language reference*?) before going on to PRACTICE.

# PRACTICE

- **Exercises 1–3**  PW/GW? In Exercise 3, if SS can't be encouraged to draw, ask them to label the outline of a person (e.g. *long, black hair*). Possibly have some pictures in reserve.

# LANGUAGE POINT 2

## Putting adjectives in the right order

Possible sequence: put the words on the board in the wrong order (e.g. *bag plastic a large*); get SS to unscramble; elicit the rule; get them to check with the *Language reference*; do the exercise and then set the exercise in the WB for homework.

## LANGUAGE POINT 3

### Possessive -s

● **Exercise 2** Each of the non-plural words must be made plural for the possessive phrase in the plural (i.e. *girl, table, a person, sister, key*). Notice that *girl* and *sister* have regular plurals but *person* is irregular. Draw attention to the reason b) and d) are different (i.e. they are non-living and can be e.g. *the table legs, the legs of the table* but not *the table's legs*). Draw attention to the punctuation (when it is *girl's* or *girls'*).

The WB exercise also revises other possessives.

● **Exercise 3** The pronunciation 'rule' ('voiced' versus 'unvoiced') is similar to that governing third person Present Simple endings and regular Past Simple endings. Possibly do some revision.

## LANGUAGE POINT 4

### Adverbs of manner

Possibly refer SS to Chapters 6 and 7 (sections 7.7 – 7.16.3) in the *Longman English Grammar* (see *Bibliography*).

The 'presentation' exercise can also be done as PW. Perhaps ask students to link the pictures to some of the words in the box. (The pictures can suggest adverbs as well as adjectives.)

Keep the PRACTICE light and amusing. You can also follow it up with the 'Adverb game' where SS take it in turns to mime an action in a particular manner, thinking of a specific adverb (e.g. scratch their head *angrily*) and other SS have to guess the adverb.

## LANGUAGE POINT 5

### Adverbs of degree

SS tend to avoid using these words or use them in a way which sounds odd. (Notice that the confusion between *very* and *too* is dealt with in Unit 8.) One problem is that some combinations don't collocate very well (e.g. we are more likely to describe a film as *incredibly violent* than *remarkably violent*). SS should start taking note of collocation.

Possibly refer SS back to the LISTENING tapescript (full edition of the SB only) for Simon talking about Emma (e.g. *she's **extremely** caring, **completely** relaxed, **extremely** bright, **very** energetic*).

In the PRACTICE do one or two as a class, to make sure SS understand. Then let them play with the possibilities (PW/GW?) and get a feeling for the best combinations.

## READING

In some ways these are more SPEAKING activities than READING activities.

At a serious level, the exercises look at stereotypical attitudes about what men/women want from each other. At the same time, it is a pity not to exploit the humorous potential of the material. For example, in the first exercise of the *Before reading* and the *Reading* you could get women SS working together in pairs before they compare their answers with the men's.

An alternative way of organising the activity: divide the class into two halves, one half reads one text, the other half the other. SS could then pair up to compare and ask e.g. *'Did the men/women think good looks were important?'*

## SPEAKING 2

Try to give each point of view equal weighting. Perhaps (in some classes) add a separate category for living together with someone of the same sex although Group A could cover that possibility. Possibly open up the discussion to e.g. couples with children who don't live together, single parents, arranged marriages, etc.

● **Exercise 2** Try to get SS to think of the pros of one of the states – even if they don't agree with it.

● **Exercise 3** An alternative is to get SS to argue their case to the whole class (from an OHT?). Possibly get SS to vote on which group argued their case most convincingly. (They are not allowed to vote for their own.)

# WRITING

## Personal letters

These contrast with the semi-formal letters in Unit 6. In personal letters we can be more idiosyncratic. However, although we convey our personality through our style, our handwriting and our overall presentation, there are still many conventions and it is easy for SS to write inappropriately.

● **Exercise 8**   It is probably best *not* to get SS to change informal language into formal language at this level.

● **Exercise 9**   Use the format of Patty's letter as a template for the SS's letter. Before SS write the letter possibly get some discussion going about the photographs of the man and write some notes on the board. Make sure they use the language of description studied earlier.

# Tapescripts

## RECORDING 1

### Robin talking about Françoise
Well, I think it was her appearance initially that attracted me. She was in her early thirties, considerably younger than me, and she'd got these big, black eyes – you know, the kind that kind of catch the light, and – very appealing – and, I also liked her long, black, curly hair and this sort of dark Mediterranean type of skin, you know – she looks more Spanish than French. And then as soon as I got to know her it was, well, just her incredibly lively personality and sense of humour. And, yes, she was such an incredibly good listener and so understanding and supportive. I, I suppose that's, what's really kept the relationship going since then is her, her character and mine seem to be so compatible.

### Françoise talking about Robin
Well, it was what you could call, actually, love at first sight. I really fancied him straight away when I saw him because, like he was tall, had blue eyes and he had a little bit of a double chin, sort of quite what we would say in French like 'well-wrapped', and he had a very charming smile as well, I remember that. Very nice voice as well, very sort of warm and, and going a little bald as well, but that … Altogether, I mean it's not features one by one that you can, you can say, you know, 'Yes, oh, the eyes are wonderful and the nose is wonderful and the lips are wonderful,' – you can't say things like that, but altogether it was, he had a type a bit like an American actor – like Paul Newman or Robert Redford or somebody like that. And physically sort of very teddy bear-like as well which is sort of very attractive, yes – very sexy.

And he was, he was a very, very funny sort of guy. Very sort of lively and contrasting to the other people around. He would always sort of crack a joke and, and be very, very open about his own life as well. He was very, straight away very friendly with me as well, and very sort of, yes, like a good old friend that I would have known for quite a long time.

### Simon talking about Emma
Well I think the thing that came over most strongly about her when I first met her was the fact that she's extremely caring and kind girl and somebody you can feel completely relaxed with when you're in her company and also a very good listener – any problems and she'll listen and make you feel a hundred per cent better. She's extremely attractive. A kind of oval face, short fairish wavy hair, big brown eyes, and gorgeous freckles, which appear when the sun is out. She's around twenty, medium height, and she's extremely bright. She's also independent, very mature. She's very energetic, likes to get up and go and do things. But she's a great girl. She's very kind, very caring. She's a lovely girl.

### Emma talking about Simon
He's got a great sense of humour. He's very funny: he likes to tell jokes. He's very romantic: he likes to send me flowers, and we go out for meals and things and he's very kind and generous. He's very intelligent. He's young: he's in his mid-twenties. He's very slim and tall, and I like tall people. He's very patient, which he needs to be with me – very responsible – if you ask him to do something you know that he'll do it, and he's very reliable like that. He's got lovely blue eyes. He's got wavy hair. He's, he's well-dressed, although he does like to wear his jeans; he's quite casual in that manner, although he's very smart when we go out. And he's, I just find him very interesting and he's just a very kind person.

## RECORDING 2

He's young: he's in his mid-twenties. He's very slim and tall. He's got lovely blue eyes. He's got wavy hair. He's well-dressed, although he does like to wear his jeans. He's quite casual in that manner, although he's very smart when we go out.

## RECORDING 3

1   both boys' sisters
2   my boss's brother
3   the cat's name
4   Hilary's friend
5   Frank's car
6   women's rights
7   the judge's (judges') decisions
8   a month's salary
9   someone else's bag
10   all actors' careers

# Key

## LISTENING

### Before listening

Couples: 1 and 2; 3 and 4.

### Listening

**1**
1 Robin
2 Françoise
3 Simon
4 Emma
5 ? (Not on the recording.)

**2**

APPEARANCE

*Françoise*: young; big, black eyes; long, black, curly hair; dark, Mediterranean type of skin – more Spanish than French.
*Robin*: tall; blue eyes; double chin; charming smile; a little bald; a bit like an American actor; very teddy bear-like; sexy.
*Emma*: attractive; kind of oval face; short, fairish, wavy hair; big, brown eyes; gorgeous freckles; medium height.
*Simon*: young – in mid-twenties; slim; tall; lovely, blue eyes; wavy hair; well-dressed; casual; smart.

PERSONALITY

*Françoise*: incredibly lively personality; sense of humour; incredibly good listener; understanding; supportive.
*Robin*: very, very funny; lively; open; friendly.
*Emma*: caring; kind; somebody you can feel relaxed with; good listener; bright; independent; mature; energetic.
*Simon*: great sense of humour; funny; tells jokes; romantic; kind; generous; intelligent; patient; reliable; interesting.

**4**
1 mid-twenties
2 slim
3 tall
4 blue
5 wavy
6 well-dressed
7 casual
8 smart

## LANGUAGE POINT 1

### Asking for descriptions

**1**
1 b)   2 c)   3 a)

## PRACTICE

**1**
ANDY:   What does your grandfather look like?
ANDY:   What's he like?
ANDY:   What does he like?

## LANGUAGE POINT 2

### Putting adjectives in the right order

a) a clever, middle-aged, Italian lawyer
b) two nice, grey, Siamese cats
c) a large, round, wooden table with a broken leg
d) an elderly, Polish woman with a lovely smile and green eyes

## LANGUAGE POINT 3

### Possessive -s

**1**
a) We add 's to the second name.
b) We use an *of*-construction.
c) We add ' after the *s*.

**2**
b) the legs of the table / the legs of the tables
c) a person's rights / people's rights
d) my sister's friends / my sisters' friends
e) the key of the doors / the keys of the doors

**3**
1 both boys' sisters (/z/)
2 my boss's brother (/ɪz/)
3 the cat's name (/s/)
4 Hilary's friend (/z/)
5 Frank's car (/s/)
6 women's rights (/z/)
7 the judge's (OR judges') decisions (/ɪz/)
8 a month's salary (/s/)
9 someone else's bag (/ɪz/)
10 all actors' careers (/z/)

## LANGUAGE POINT 4

### Adverbs of manner

*Adjectives*: rude, angry, quiet, friendly, serious, perfect
*Adverbs*: loudly, carefully, badly, quickly, cleverly, lively, softly, nervously
*Adjectives and adverbs*: straight, slow (*adjective* and sometimes *adverb*), hard

## LANGUAGE POINT 5

### Adverbs of degree

**1**
a bit, rather, quite, a little, fairly, pretty, on the … side

**2**
extremely, incredibly, really, terribly, remarkably

**3**
*highest*: extremely, incredibly
*smallest*: a bit, a little

## PRACTICE

**1**
Possible answers:
a) I'm *terribly* bored.
b) This car is *quite* fast.
c) It's *rather* a violent film.
d) She's *on the* lazy *side*.
e) They speak English *really* badly.

# READING

## Reading

**2**

A

1 man/husband
2 women/wives
3 women/wives
4 women/wives
5 women/wives

B

1 men  2 woman  3 men  4 women  5 men
6 woman  7 women  8 men  9 women  10 men
11 men  12 men  13 woman  14 women

# WRITING

## Personal letters

**1**

(7) 11 Castle St.

(1) 11th March 1991

(2) Dear Kate,

(9) Hello, dear. Sorry I haven't written earlier. I've been meaning to but it seems every time I get a quiet moment to put pen to paper the phone rings and I have to go to help with some recording.

(6) I haven't got much news. After a pretty exciting three weeks' holiday, it's back to work non-stop. Steve and I hardly ever see each other at the moment. I've also taken to serious volleyball training: two hours every weekend evening, especially difficult as I have to get out of bed to be at the studios by 7 a.m.! I was working evenings before Christmas, but I had to change to fit in the volleyball.

(4) Enough of me telling you how busy I am. The big question is when are you two coming to stay – we're dying to see you!? The spare room now has a bed so no excuses. Why don't you try and make it before the winter? Give us a ring anyway.

(8) Must rush – as always. 'Bye, and please give Phil a hug from me. I miss you both a lot.

(3) Love,

Patty

(5) PS Thanks for the card.

**2**

Patty wants to invite Kate to come and stay.

**3**

a) 6  b) 4  c) 8  d) 9

**4**

a) Patty works at a recording studio and she's very busy.
b) She likes exciting holidays and playing volleyball.

**5**

All the best; Best wishes; See you; Cheers; Regards; Love.

**6**

*Similarities*: e.g. both have the writer's address in the top right-hand corner; both divide the text into paragraphs.

*Differences*: e.g. the addressee's name is not included; the style is more informal and personal ('Hello, dear.'); the sentences are incomplete ('Must rush – as always.').

**7**

I refer to your letter of the 19th March.
I am grateful for your assistance.
I apologise for the delay in replying.

**8**

You know you wrote on the 19th March?
Thanks for helping me.
Sorry I didn't get back to you sooner.

# A place to live

## Students' Book

**General theme:** people and places.
**Unit topic:** homes.

**READING:** a magazine article about a room.
**VOCABULARY:** making opposites using prefixes and suffixes.
**PRONUNCIATION:** syllables and word stress.

**LANGUAGE POINT 1:** prepositions of place.
**LANGUAGE POINT 2:** comparative and superlative forms.
**LANGUAGE POINT 3:** *very / too / not enough.*

**SPEAKING:** discussing photographs of unusual places; mini-roleplay.
**WRITING:** linking expressions which join clauses within sentences, and connect ideas across sentences; writing a description of a room or a house.

## Workbook

**LISTENING:** interview with an estate agent.
**GRAMMAR:** comparison of adjectives and adverbs; superlatives; prepositions of place and direction.
**VOCABULARY:** furniture and household objects; doing things in the house; forming adjectives; prefixes.
**WRITING:** linking expressions.

## Language

The main language focus in this unit is on comparative and superlative forms of adjectives and adverbs. It therefore revises and extends work done on adjectives and adverbs in the previous unit. The unit also practises prepositions of place, and adverbs such as *very, too* and *enough*.

Students will probably not have any 'conceptual' problems with comparative forms (although the differences between *very, too* and *not enough* can be difficult for some SS), but most speakers of non-western European languages find forming this construction quite difficult. Comparatives are often formed differently in their own language, and so SS often translate literally. In Japanese, for example, there is no inflection, and in Farsi the comparative/superlative is always formed by the addition of a suffix.

### Common problems
#### Comparative and superlative forms

**1** Not knowing when to use *more* or *-er*. Spanish and Thai speakers, for example, use *more* and *most* in their own language and so tend to translate directly, e.g. \**The river is more long.* or \**The river is more dirtier.*

**2** SS are not always able to work out how many syllables there are in a word when looking at the 'rules' (see the *Language reference*). See the PRONUNCIATION section of this unit for work in this area.

**3** Irregular forms (e.g. *good, bad, far*) need to be learned by SS – they are a frequent source of error (\**It's badder than yours.*).

**4** Spelling can be a problem (\**It is prettyer by the sea than in the country.*), although previous work on spelling (see Review Unit 4) will help (i.e. doubling consonants, and changing *y* to *i*).

**5** *As* and *than* can be problematic. For example, in French, the word for *that* is used: \**It was colder* ***as*** *yesterday* or … *colder* ***that*** *yesterday.*

**6**  SS often get confused about when to use the subject or object pronoun (*She's older than I am.* or *She's older than me.*). Both are acceptable in everyday English, although some people still prefer the (strictly correct) subject pronoun. Discourage SS from saying *She's older than I.*

**7**  Many SS often miss out *the* when talking about superlatives (*It is longest river in the world.*). Also SS often say (*The most expensive painting **of** the world.*).

### Very / too / not enough

SS often get confused between the meaning of *very* and *too* : e.g. *I like it.* *It is too nice.* or *It's very too nice.*

Very is often put in front of comparatives instead of *much/far.* *He is very cleverer than me.* *Very* can be used in front of *-est* superlatives (*the very cleverest*) but not in front of *the most* (*the very most beautiful*).

Note that *very* cannot go in front of all adjectives (for more information on this see section 7.51 in the *Longman English Grammar* – details in the *Bibliography*).

# READING

## Before reading

Tell SS that the text they are going to read, *A Room of My Own*, is part of a magazine series where people talk about their favourite rooms. This will be a lead-in to the discussion in Exercises 1 and 2, which should also generate *furniture* vocabulary (for more on this see the WB). You could also ask SS to look at the photograph of Ivan's room and give their views on it.

## Reading

● **Exercises 1 and 2**  The aim is reading comprehension. Use the photograph to introduce some of the vocabulary that SS might have difficulty with (e.g. *retriever, seaman's chest*, etc.) and perhaps elicit from SS where you can buy furniture from (to elicit *jumble sale* and *market*). Give SS a time limit to read the text and get oral feedback. You might like to pick up on the use of *tended to* in the second paragraph (this also comes up a lot in the LISTENING in the WB).

● **Exercises 3 and 4**  Focus on one of the language points of the unit (i.e. prepositional phrases). These exercises could be followed up by LANGUAGE POINT 1 for more work on prepositions of place. Further practice in the WB.

● **Exercise 5**  Draws SS' attention to a fairly standard way of constructing a paragraph, which can be used as a model when analysing other texts.

# VOCABULARY

## Making opposites

A good opportunity to make SS aware of some of the most common prefixes and suffixes in English and how this helps them to recognise opposites. Get SS to brainstorm the ones they know in groups, and then introduce the ones they don't know. Draw their attention to these in any subsequent reading texts and encourage SS to make notes of opposites and also 'word families' (as in the example in Exercise 3) in their vocabulary books. Make it clear that not all adjectives take such prefixes and suffixes (e.g. *nice*) and that there are not always direct opposites.

# PRONUNCIATION

## Syllables and word stress

SS were introduced to syllables in Unit 6 but this exercise provides further practice in breaking up words into syllables and identifying the main stress. Extra work with SS on checking syllables and word stress in a good dictionary is also useful. The *Longman Dictionary of Contemporary English* shows word stress and syllables.

● **Exercise 2**  Make three columns on the board headed *Two syllables*, *Three syllables* and *Four syllables*. After SS have had time to work on the activity in pairs, elicit which words go in which columns. Possibly encourage them to check their answers in the dictionary before giving you the answers. This activity could be extended at this point and on future occasions to include and revise words which SS have recently met.

# LANGUAGE POINT 1

## Saying where things are

● **Exercise 1, a)**  An alternative is to get SS to 'brainstorm' vocabulary before they listen – ask them to predict what you would expect to find in a kitchen if you were renting a flat. Monitor SS' pronunciation and spelling. SS could then check off which things Melanie mentions, and add any others.

● **Exercise 1, b)**  The listening text revises use of prepositions. After SS have completed the listening task get them to check their diagrams in pairs. Alternatively, put the diagram on the board and then get SS to come to the board and label it, based on what they heard, or complete the diagram yourself, based on a class consensus. It may well be that SS are not sure how certain prepositions are used and these will need presenting. You may also want to include other prepositions of place (see sections 8.6–8 in the *Longman English Grammar* – details in the *Bibliography*).

● **Exercise 2**  There is an opportunity here to do some work on contrastive stress: '*It isn't under the stairs, it's next to the freezer.*' PW? You could extend this to describing other rooms familiar to all SS (e.g. the classroom).

# PRACTICE

● **Exercises 1 and 2**  A variation of 'Describe and draw'. Notice we suggest that SS label the drawings – obviously the more artistically inclined SS could draw the articles instead.

An alternative to Exercises 1 and 2 is to bring in magazine pictures of a room. Student A describes a room to Student B, who draws it. Or Student B is given the items of furniture cut from the picture, and has to arrange the picture according to how Student A describes it. This avoids the need for drawing, which some SS do not like. Make notes on SS' use of prepositions (and also adjective order, when they are describing possessions), for further practice later.

● **Exercise 3**  Possibly get SS to bring in their own possessions or photographs.

# LANGUAGE POINT 2

## Making comparisons

● **Exercise 1**  Practises comparative forms with *-er*, using SS' general knowledge. Focus on contrastive stress and weak forms (e.g. /ðən/) here. (This could, of course, be extended into a class quiz, with SS producing the questions, using reference books to help, and asking each other questions in teams.)

● **Exercise 3**  Practises comparative forms with *more* and *less*. It requires SS' opinions – there is no 'right' answer. Possibly get SS to think of other examples.

● **Exercise 5**  Focus on the weak form (/əz/ … /əz/) and point out that *not so … as* is also possible.

The gap-fill exercises should be used in conjunction with the *Language reference*. Remind SS to put new items in their personalised grammar books.

# PRACTICE

● **Exercise 1**  Further ideas for practising these constructions can be found in the handbook, *Grammar Practice Activities* (see *Bibliography*), from which this activity has been adapted. This activity could be done as PW/GW.

● **Exercise 2**  Possibly extend this into a 'desert island' type activity – i.e. each student saying which six (for example) things he or she would take to a desert island, and why.

● **Exercise 3**  Warn SS that these expressions can sometimes sound a little bit old-fashioned. However, they are good practice of the structure, and fun, and SS may well come across some of them (e.g. in literature) even if they themselves don't use them.

## LANGUAGE POINT 3

### *Very / too / not enough*

The main focus here is on *very* to emphasise an adjective, and on *too / not enough* (see the *Language reference*). You might also want to introduce the idea of *much too / far too* (e.g. *small*) for emphasis.

## SPEAKING

● **Exercise 1**   Could be extended by using more photographs. Get SS to think of other unusual forms of accommodation, and their pros and cons.

An alternative activity would be for SS to design an advert 'selling' one of these places and see which is the most convincing. House adverts from English-language newspapers could prove an interesting model.
   A possible link is different types of houses that people live in. Possibly use the interview with an estate agent and the vocabulary area of houses (*bungalow, cottage*, etc.) – both in the WB – in class or direct SS' attention towards it. There is also scope for further vocabulary work on buying and renting houses (*mortgage, deposit*, etc.).

## WRITING

### Linking expressions

● **Exercises 1 and 2**   The aim is to revise and extend linking expressions introduced in Review Unit 3, and to focus on their grammatical use in a sentence (see the *Language reference*). Possibly explain the differences between clauses and sentences (see the *Language reference* in Unit 6). It is worth spending time on linking expressions to help SS write more coherently and in longer sentences. There is more work on this in the WB.

● **Exercise 3**   After SS have written the draft they could give it to their partner to look at and comment on before they write their final version. Impress upon SS the need to monitor their / each other's work for linking expressions and prepositional phrases studied in this unit.

# Tapescript

## RECORDING 1

MELANIE: … and the living room overlooks a pond.
JULIE:  Well, that sounds OK. What about the kitchen, though? What's that like?
M:  It's not too bad as I remember. You go in the door and there's a window opposite with a fairly large sink underneath, and draining boards on each side. Oh, the cooker is next to the sink, on the right, in the corner.
J:  Is there a washing machine?
M:  Yes, under the stairs. The stairs lead up from the kitchen. And there's a freezer, too – a small one, on top of the fridge. Oh, the fridge is next to the washing machine, by the way.
J:  Lots of space to put things?
M:  Oh, enough, I think. Oh, there are shelves over the cooker. And I think there's a cupboard on the floor between the table and the cooker.  Oh, and there's a round table in the middle of the room, with four chairs, to eat at, and another table opposite the window, as you go in, on the right in the corner, that we can work at.

# Key

## READING

### Reading

**1**
He lives in a flat in London. He is a window cleaner and an actor, and is gentle and enthusiastic.

**2**
a) By looking through customers' windows while cleaning windows.
b) He is a window cleaner and an actor. He has been a fireman.
c) To buy his flat from the council.
e) The money he lives on.

**3**
b) the Persian rug: in a carpet sale; on the floor, in the middle of the room.
c) the sofa: he bought it; on the left of the room.
d) the Victorian chair: he bought it; next to the chest.
e) the plants: from his mother and Columbia Road flower market; in front of the window, in the corner, and behind the television.
f) the television table: Bermondsey market; in the corner, near the window.
g) the wooden dog: from his girlfriend; on the television.
h) the African figure: Dar-es-Salaam; on the coffee table.
i) the pictures: a jumble sale; on the wall, above the chest.
j) the tips: his job; in the gin bottle, on the coffee table.

**4**
Example answers:
in: *in the sitting room*; *in a carpet sale*; *in Holland*
through: *through his customers' windows*
at: *at a Sunday jumble sale*
on: *on a cut-down Victorian table*

**5**
a) It gives more detailed information and an example of the inspiration he gets by looking through customers' windows.
b) It introduces the topic of his flat, and specifically the sitting room, which is described in the rest of the article.

## VOCABULARY

### Making opposites

**1**
a) impractical, useless, untidy, colourless, unromantic, tasteless

**2**
unnecessary, inexperienced, insensitive, dislike, disagree, irresponsibly, impatiently, unpleasant, illogically, tactlessly, dishonest, unmarried

**4**
a) irresponsible   b) inexperienced   c) pleasant
d) disagree   e) dishonestly   f) tactfully

## PRONUNCIATION

### Syllables and word stress

**1**
a) Four
b) The third syllable

## LANGUAGE POINT 1

### Saying where things are

**1**
a) washing machine; fridge; freezer; table; chair; cupboard; shelf; sink; draining board; cooker.
b)

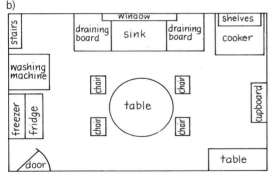

**2**
There are seven more differences.
–  The cooker isn't next to the sink; it's under the stairs.
–  The freezer isn't on top of the fridge; it's on the right, in the corner, near the washing machine.
–  The fridge isn't next to the washing machine; it's near the window.
–  The shelves aren't over the cooker; they are above the freezer.
–  The cupboard is on the right as you go in the door, against the wall.
–  There isn't a round table in the middle of the room; the table (which is square) and four chairs are in the right corner.
–  There isn't a second table.

## LANGUAGE POINT 2

### Making comparisons

**1**
a) False. (China is smaller than the USSR.)
b) True.
c) False. (The North Sea is colder than the Mediterranean Sea.)
d) True.
e) False. (The USA have a worse football team than Brazil.)
f) False. (In Britain it becomes dark later in summer than in winter.)

**2**
*-(e)r; better; earlier*

**4**
*more, less*

**5**
*as, as*

**6**
b)  *-(e)st, most, least*

## PRACTICE

**3**
b) sin   c) a post   d) a peacock   e) a sheet   f) nails
g) gold   h) a button

## PRACTICE

*Very / too / not enough*

1  He's too tall to get in the house.
2  There isn't enough petrol.
3  It's too hot (to drink).
4  She's not old enough to go in. (She's too young to go in.)

## WRITING

### Linking expressions

**1**
a) Before   b) when / as soon as   c) while/when
d) while/whereas

**2**
a) too / as well   b) Meanwhile   c) However   d) Then

# Reading the signs

## Students' Book

**General theme:** the future.
**Unit topic:** signs and predictions.

**LISTENING 1:** a radio expert talking about the significance of itches.
**LANGUAGE POINT 1:** open/first conditionals (making predictions).
**LANGUAGE POINT 2:** levels of certainty (*likely, probably*, etc., *may, might, could*).

**VOCABULARY:** signs of illness (symptoms, illnesses, cures); antonyms and synonyms.
**LANGUAGE POINT 3:** *unless*.
**LANGUAGE POINT 4:** promises and threats (*If you ...; Unless you ...*).
**LANGUAGE POINT 5:** warnings (*if/unless*).

**LISTENING 2:** a palm reader reading a man's palm.
**SPEAKING:** telling a story from cues.
**WRITING:** paragraphing / writing a narrative.

## Workbook

**READING:** article about superstitions.
**GRAMMAR:** open conditionals (including *unless*); asking open conditional questions; certainty and possibility (*will, may/might, could, probably, maybe*).
**VOCABULARY:** health; synonyms; antonyms.
**PRONUNCIATION:** word stress.

## Language

This unit introduces open (or 'first') conditionals, although SS of this level will probably have some familiarity with them (*will* has been practised in Unit 5). *Unless* is often a problem for many SS. The unit also looks at modals in relation to levels of certainty. While most nationalities have equivalents of both in their language some problems of interference occur.

The main problem for SS with modals is when to use them and the overuse of some modals at the expense of others. There is also a tendency to follow the modal with a *to*-infinitive: *\*She can to swim.*

## Common problems
### Open conditionals

**1**  Some nationalities (e.g. Russian and Hindi speakers) tend to use *will* in both clauses: *\*If you will pass the exam, I'll ...* On the other hand Portuguese speakers use the Present Simple in both clauses: *\*If you pass, I buy you ...* There is more work on time expressions + the present tense in Unit 10.

**2**  Thai speakers often omit *if* and German speakers frequently confuse *if* (theoretical) and *when* (definite) – also practised in Unit 10.

### Modal auxiliaries

**1**  Arabic, unlike most other languages, has no modal equivalents: *\*It may that it rain. \*Does she can swim?*

**2**  SS may be familiar with *may* for 'permission' (which may confuse) but are likely to say *\*It can rain tomorrow.*

# LISTENING 1

## Listening

A lot of vocabulary related to parts of the body is required both here and in the VOCABULARY section later. Make sure SS revise parts of the body (e.g. WB exercise, Unit 7). Here they will need: *shoulder, elbow, knee, lips*. Explain *itch* and *scratch*.

● **Exercises 1 and 2**   Prediction exercises.

● **Exercise 3**   Explain the pun in the recording: 'Is Our Future up to Scratch?' Explain words like *ancients* and *promotion*. Point out an example of an open conditional (e.g. *... if it's on the right side, you will meet a female stranger.*) as a lead-in to Exercise 4.

# PRACTICE

## Open conditionals: making predictions

Possibly use horoscopes for further practice (e.g. *'If your star sign is Cancer, you will make a new friend.'*). Note the WB exercise includes *unless* – not practised until later in the unit.

# LANGUAGE POINT 2

## Levels of certainty

This exercise contrasts the idea of definiteness in *will* with possibility in *may/might/could*. Explain the meaning of *likely/unlikely*. Notice that *probably* modifies the definiteness of *will* (practised in Unit 5 – perhaps do some revision).

# VOCABULARY

## Signs of illness

● **Exercise 1**   PW. If you want speaker A to be Student A, alternate SS because speaker A has more gaps to complete than B. As far as possible, get SS to guess the answers from context. If you do personalised follow-up (e.g. *'Have you ever had food poisoning?'*) be careful not to force embarrassing revelations. Possibly practise the pronunciation of the vocabulary.

● **Exercise 2**   Could be expanded into a roleplay (PW), where Student A complains (e.g. *'My throat's terribly sore.'*) and Student B responds (e.g. *'Try these pastilles.'*). Could also be extended into other complaints (e.g. a broken ankle) and revision or presentation of other ways of giving advice (e.g. *Why don't you ... ? You'd better ... ? I think you should ...*). (See also WB.)

## Antonyms and synonyms

Refer SS to the *Language reference*. They need to be aware of the problems of connotation (that similar words can suggest different feelings) and collocation (that a word's antonym/synonym depends on the lexical context).

● **Exercise 1**   Possibly do extra work with dictionaries (e.g. look up other meanings of *dry, strong, hard*).

● **Exercise 3**   These words link to Exercises 1 and 2 above. One idea is to put them on the board and ask SS to come up and write as many adjectives next to each as they can.

# LANGUAGE POINT 3

## *Unless*

At an intermediate level, point out that *unless* normally means *if... not* (a better definition would be 'except on the condition that'). However, as the *Language reference* points out, they are not always interchangeable. (See sections 14, 20.2–3 in the *Longman English Grammar* for more details.)

# LANGUAGE POINT 4

## Promises and threats

As with *Predictions* (LANGUAGE POINT 1), this is a functional heading to practise formal accuracy of *if* and *unless* and recognise intention from intonation. Notice that the pitch on promises is sometimes higher and the tone often less intense than with threats. Perhaps allow SS to practise this themselves.

# LANGUAGE POINT 5

## Warnings

Another functional heading in order to provide practice. In PRACTICE Exercise 2 make sure SS imagine themselves in the situation and actually try to threaten or promise. PRACTICE Exercise 3 c) provides freer discussion where the structures should come up fairly naturally.

# LISTENING 2

## Before listening

Treat this activity lightly. Be careful of any sensitivities SS might have about touching or looking at each others' hands. Check vocabulary: *palm, wrist, index finger, thumb.*

## Listening

The palm-reading here was genuine. The 'reader' had no idea beforehand about the person whose palm she read. The subject said her analysis was accurate. Do the exercises as PW/GW?

Notice that the palm reader mentions the following directly: *the mind line, the fate line, the health line.* She also refers to other features of the hand (e.g. *strong thumb*). Possibly help with some of the vocabulary: *lack of imagination, straightforward, close, doubtful, artistic streak, nasty temper, prone to headaches, break up, play you up a bit, on the mend.* Point out the use of *pretty* and *slightly.*

# SPEAKING

## Story telling

Possible lines of development: a fortune teller predicted (there was an unlucky omen?) the man would be mugged *or* would have a heart attack because he eats/drinks too much and is unfit.

● **Exercise 2** Have a rehearsal phase where SS focus on ideas and fluency before getting the story as accurate as possible. Also invent dialogue? SS could then mime their story to other groups and get them to guess the outline. Finally, groups could present their story to other groups or the class (on tape? on video?). Be warned, though, much of the story has been given away in the cues so, for prediction exercises to work and interest to be maintained, stories must be imaginative.

# WRITING

## Writing narrative

The precise sequence of events is given in these short sentences, so tell SS the main aim is sentence/paragraph construction. However, the story is very bare (e.g. with few adjectival/adverbial phrases) and needs to be made a bit more dramatic. Help SS by giving them some questions to think about: e.g. *Who were A and B? What was their relationship / their ages? Where were they on holiday? Describe the place, the weather, the hotel.* etc.

There are many possible ways of dividing the sentences into four or five groups – depends how much SS want to expand certain sections. (Compare work on paragraph development in Unit 8.)

Possibly, do the first few sentences on the board to show how simple sentences are joined and made complex or more dramatic (e.g. *Adam and Ben had been good friends for many years. After three wasted years at university they left to get a job but decided, rightly or wrongly, to go ...* etc.).

Allow SS to draft the story and get suggested improvements from other SS before redrafting.

# Tapescripts

## RECORDING 1

ANNOUNCER: Have you got an itch? If so, it could be that your body is trying to tell you something. In this morning's programme Peter Marsh asks the question: 'Is Our Future up to Scratch?'

PETER MARSH: According to the ancients, when a little bodily irritation occurs – suddenly and for no apparent reason – it can be a sign of something to come. For example, if you want to scratch your head, it's generally a good sign. If the itch is on the top of your head, you'll probably get promotion in your job. If it's on the right side, you will meet a female stranger – on the left, it will be a man. Itches to other parts of the body are signs too. If your right shoulder suddenly irritates you, you will receive a large sum of money. But if it is your left shoulder, unhappiness is sure to follow. As for the elbow, an itchy right elbow means you'll hear good news but if it's the left it means bad news. And watch out if you get a strong desire to scratch your knees. It means you'll soon be jealous of someone. But you will soon make a happy journey if it's the right knee and an unpleasant journey if it's the left. As for the lips …

## RECORDING 2

a) Unless you fly us to America, we'll blow up the plane.
b) If you score a goal in tomorrow's final, I'll give you a £100 bonus.
c) I'll lend you my car if you let me borrow your motorbike.
d) We'll take away all your furniture unless you pay us now.
e) If you don't help me carry this ladder, my brother won't give you a lift home.

## RECORDING 3

PALM READER: Don't take anything that I say too personally. I'm just only telling you what I see. I mean I may be totally wrong but … it's a very straight mind line which shows a slight lack of imagination. You're pretty straightforward in your thinking and your emotions are pretty straightforward. Your fate line is slightly off in the early days. It looks as if you, your early family life wasn't too good. Almost, it just feels like there was a breaking away of the family, either that your parents were divorced or there was problem, there were problems in the family so you weren't terribly close to them. … There was a very … well, it looks as if you've been married … from … quite early actually … twenty-five? … But there was also a relationship, it was very strong, with an older woman? … You have two children? … And there was, or will be another one? … Well, I say 'was' because it's slightly doubtful. … You, … I don't know; I don't know what your job is, but I mean obviously you've been gardening today but, … there's an artistic streak there somewhere. … You didn't do, do you paint? Or you write? … Your very long little finger, so you're obviously … Yes, you write, or you do write, or … poetry or something. … Something in that area. … It's artistic anyway. … You've got a good strong thumb. … bit stubborn. … You've got a bit of a nasty temper … little bit unsure of

yourself in some areas. I mean, better, better now but as a child you were obviously very, very shy but I've got a feeling that was something to do with your family life, your family background. … But you're a bit more sure of yourself now. … But you have doubts about yourself. … Very attracted to the opposite sex. … Health line: again that's a break-up in your early days but that could have been emotional. … Again I just get this feeling it was something to do with your family, but so … your health line was slightly broken up, got better as you got to late teens. … Prone to headaches. … And you'll be needing glasses I should imagine. … Your eyesight's beginning to play you up a bit. … And also chest infections. … Sorry, you're not going to be a rich man. Oh, you'll be all right. You're not going to be a rich man because you quite like spending it. … But in fact it looks as if you've gone through financial troubles for about four or five years, but they're getting better. Things will get better. In fact they're on the mend now.

# Key

## LISTENING 1

### Before listening

**1**

In Britain the following are normally thought of as bringing good luck: a rabbit's foot (if you carry it with you); a horseshoe (they are sometimes put over the front door of the house); crossing fingers.

The following are normally thought of as bringing you bad luck: spilling salt (so throw it over your left shoulder if you spill it – this prevents bad luck); breaking a mirror; Friday 13th (but some people think 13 is a lucky number; in Japan 4 and 9 are unlucky whereas in Italy 17 is unlucky).

### Listening

**1**

They are scratching because they have an itch.

**2**

Good luck: 2 and 3
Bad luck: 1 and 4

**4**

a) the left side of your head
b) the right shoulder
c) the right elbow
d) the left knee

## LANGUAGE POINT 1

### Open conditionals: making predictions

a) ii) and iii)
b) Present Simple comes after *If*. We cannot say *If the itch will be* …
c) The second clause.
d) There is no difference in meaning.

You can also use *may*, *might* and *could* in the second clause.

## PRACTICE

**1**
a) If your hand itches, you'll (may/might/could) get rich.
b) Somebody will invite you out if you have an itchy tummy.
c) If you want to scratch your right eye, you'll see an old friend.
d) If you have an itch on the lips, you'll kiss someone soon.
e) Someone will say rude things about you behind your back if you want to scratch your left ear.
f) If your right cheek itches, you'll soon receive praise.

**2**
Examples:
If you walk under a ladder, something bad will happen to you.
If you see a pin and pick it up, you will have good luck.
If you put an umbrella up indoors, you will have bad luck.
If you see a black cat walking in front of you, something nice will happen to you. (Black cats are unlucky in many countries.)
If you hang a bag of garlic around your neck, you will keep away illness.
If you get to the end of a rainbow, you will find a pot of gold.
If you pull a wishbone and you get the biggest bit, your wish will come true.

## LANGUAGE POINT 2

### Levels of certainty

**1**
b) you'll probably have
c) you might become a journalist / you could become / you may also be
d) you probably won't
e) you won't live

## VOCABULARY

### Signs of illness

**1 and 2**
a) A: throat's *sore* / don't *cough* at all
   B: like *tonsillitis*
   *Advice*: Suck some throat pastilles.
b) A: can't stop *sneezing* / high *temperature*
   B: probably *flu*
   *Advice*: Go to bed. Keep warm. Have a hot lemon drink.
c) A: very *sick* / terrible *diarrhoea*
   B: suffered from *food poisoning*
   *Advice*: Don't try to eat anything. Drink lots of water. See a doctor.
d) A: this *cut* / wouldn't stop *bleeding*
   B: kind of *infection*
   *Advice*: Rub on an antiseptic lotion. Put a plaster or tie a bandage on it.
e) A: very *faint* / terrible *pain*
   B: have a *heart attack*
   *Advice*: Get more exercise. Eat less fat.

### Antonyms and synonyms

**1**
a) sweet  b) mild  c) easy  d) thin  e) interesting
f) dull  g) heavy  h) poor  i) hard  j) return  k) single

**2**
Examples:
a) good-looking/handsome
b) funny
c) good/enjoyable
d) mischievous/naughty
e) soft
f) foolish/stupid

**3**
Examples:
a) cold, mild, wet, hot, dry, humid, nice, horrible
b) mild, strong, hard, soft, foreign
c) hard, easy, interesting, difficult
d) hard, soft, bumpy, comfortable, long, short, narrow
e) interesting, dull, long, short, funny, strange

## LANGUAGE POINT 3

*Unless*

**1**
a) Yes.
b) Yes.
c) If … not.

## LANGUAGE POINT 4

### Promises and threats

**1**
a) If you don't clean my car, I won't take you to a football match.
b) Unless you hurry up, I'll go without you.
c) If you increase my pay, I won't look for another job.

**2**
Sentences i) and c) are promises; ii), iii) and a) and b) are threats.

**3**
a) Threat  b) Promise  c) Promise  d) Threat  e) Threat

## LANGUAGE POINT 5

### Warnings

a) Yes.
b) Yes.
   They tell (warn) the other person of the probable (unpleasant) result of the action in the *if/unless* clause.

## PRACTICE

**1**
a) If you don't slow down, I'll never …
b) Unless you stop that, I'll send …
c) If you don't quieten down, I'll kick …
d) Unless you clean up this mess, you can't …
e) I'll send it to you if you give me …

**3**
a) 1 The young man is trying to light a fire in the forest. The forest might catch fire.
   2 The girl is about to try to walk across a frozen pond. The ice might break and she might fall into the water.
   3 The woman on the left is about to take a large number of pills. She might become addicted to them.
   4 The young man is lying on the beach in the hot sun. He could get sunstroke.
b) 1 If you light a fire there, the whole forest will catch fire.
   2 If you step on there, you'll fall through the ice.
   3 If you take any more tranquillisers, you'll get addicted to them.
   4 If you lie there much longer, you'll get sunstroke.

## LISTENING 2

### Listening

**1**
a) The straight mind line.
b) The fate line which was a little off in the early days.
c) The long finger.
d) The strong thumb.
e) The health line.

**2**
a) Shy as a child.
b) Can be bad-tempered.
c) Attracted to women.
d) Not close to parents.
e) Married in twenties.
f) Headaches.

**3**
a), b) and c)

# A better life?

## Students' Book

**General theme:** the future.
**Unit topic:** houses of the future.

**READING:** magazine text about houses of the future; introductory listening extract.
**LANGUAGE POINT 1:** time conjunctions (*as soon as*, *when*, etc.) + the present.
**LANGUAGE POINT 2:** *if* and *when*.
**LANGUAGE POINT 3:** Future Passive.
**LANGUAGE POINT 4:** making personal arrangements – Present Continuous for future time.

**PRONUNCIATION:** vowel sounds; using the phonemic chart.
**VOCABULARY:** phrasal verbs with *up* and *down*.

**SPEAKING:** discussion of what people will look like in the future.
**CREATIVE WRITING:** comparing style of magazine text with short story; continuing the story.

## Workbook

**LISTENING:** interviews with people about the future.
**GRAMMAR:** time clauses; *if* or *when*; future forms; Future Passive.
**VOCABULARY:** phrasal verbs with *on* and *off*; phrasal verbs with *take*; describing objects.
**WRITING:** spelling.

## Language

The language points in this unit are mainly connected to future time. SS' main problems will probably be with the correct form and remembering to use it. They will have been exposed to most, if not all of the points before but now need practice in using them.

Phrasal verbs, also introduced in this unit, pose more of a problem as they do not exist in many languages.

## Common problems

### Time conjunctions

A typical mistake is *I'll phone you when he will arrive*. In Latin languages conjunctions of time with future reference are followed by a future form.

### If and when

Some nationalities get confused between the different meanings (hypothetical and definite) between *if* and *when* (see the *Language reference*). *If* is commonly used for *when* and vice versa, e.g. in German and West African languages.

### Future Passive

SS often get confused with the formation of the passive, e.g. *It will be making of glass*. (See Unit 19.)

### Present Continuous

For SS whose mother tongue has no Present Continuous form (e.g. French and Russian) the use of the Present Continuous for future reference poses great difficulty. However, in most languages the Present Simple for future reference is commonly used more than in English.

There is also confusion between the Present Continuous and *going to* + base form (see the *Language reference* for the difference). Make it clear to SS when *going to* and the Present Continuous can be used interchangeably (e.g. *They're going to buy / They're buying a new car tomorrow.*) and when not (e.g. *It's raining tomorrow.*).

## Phrasal verbs

Most SS find it difficult to accept that the addition of a particle can change the meaning of a verb.

SS find it difficult to know how to use the different types of phrasal verbs grammatically – for example, when the verb can be separated from the particle by the object and when it can't (see Unit 15).

# READING

## Before reading

● **Exercise 1**   Revises *will* (see Unit 5). Encourage SS to use modals as possibility (e.g. *may, might* and *could*) – revision from Unit 9.

● **Exercise 2**   Opportunity for revision of comparative forms. Possibly get SS to predict what houses in the future will be like before they listen to David speaking. Notice that in the listening there are examples of *will* as well as *when* + the present tense.

## Reading

● **Exercises 1 and 2**   Elicit the vocabulary for other things in the picture, introducing new items as necessary. Then encourage SS to read the text quickly to find the details of what is shown in the picture.

● **Exercise 4**   SS could use their dictionaries to check whether the word they have decided on is correct.

● **Exercise 6**   SS could also draw their ideal home of the future.

# LANGUAGE POINT 1

## Time conjunctions

SS have already been introduced to linking expressions. This exercise aims to illustrate the use of the present tense which follows them when referring to the present or the future.

# PRACTICE

The two exercises practise the use of time conjunctions in both a controlled and personalised way. PW/GW?

# LANGUAGE POINT 2

## *If* or *when*?

● **Exercise 1**   SS should be encouraged to work the 'rule' out for themselves.

● **Exercise 2**   Get SS to discuss the reasons why some of the sentences are impossible.

# LANGUAGE POINT 3

## Future Passive

The passive for the verb forms studied in this book is dealt with in Unit 19. Here the passive with *will* is focused on in isolation and in the context of a formal letter. The justification for this appearing early is that it comes up naturally in the text and is not difficult conceptually for SS to grasp.

# PRACTICE

● **Exercise 1**   Possibly discuss why *will* has been used instead of *going to* (revision of Unit 5)?

● **Exercise 3**   Revision of formal letter style (see Unit 6).

● **Exercise 4**   SS should discuss *why* one sentence is more appropriate than the other and get some feeling as to what connotation the passive has, when to use it, and to what effect.

● **Exercise 5**   Change the title of the conference if you think another topic would interest your SS more. The important thing is to provide a situation where SS will practise future forms.

## LANGUAGE POINT 4

### Making arrangements

SS may need to be told why the Present Continuous is sometimes used in preference to *going to* (see the *Language reference*).

## PRACTICE

Draw SS' attention to how you make notes in diaries, so that SS do not write whole sentences. If you like, suggest that they complete the diaries based on their real plans for, for example, the following week. An alternative to this would be to give SS copies of diaries already prepared so that there is a definite 'solution' to the problem.

## PRONUNCIATION

### Vowels

Point out the difference between vowel letters (*a e i o u*) and the twelve vowel sounds.

● **Exercise 1** SS should practise the sounds in pairs. Individual students should then read out one sound in front of the class. Point out the difference between long and short vowels, and the two dots which indicate the long vowels. If appropriate, explain to SS how the sound is made. Tell them that the lips are open for all vowels, and that all vowels are 'voiced', but the shape of the lips and position of the jaw and tongue will be different depending on the sound. (See books such as *Ship or Sheep?* – details in *Bibliography* – for diagrams of the mouth when making these sounds.) Try to make it into a 'fun' activity, and get SS to exaggerate the sounds. If possible, SS should be given follow-up work to do in the language laboratory, as practising vowel sounds is something, once introduced, that can best be done by SS on their own. This is particularly important if SS come from different countries, as it is difficult to focus adequately on all the different problem sounds in the classroom. There is follow-up work on vowel sounds in Unit 11 in the WB.

● **Exercise 2** Encourage SS to use the phonemic chart (either the one on SB page 149, or a chart in the classroom) to interpret the sounds. They shouldn't see it as a test of what they know, but as practice in using the chart and being able to find out pronunciation even when the T is not there.

● **Exercise 3** Possibly stop after each word and allow SS to discuss with each other and consult the chart. Don't let them be 'put off' by phonemic symbols – make it fun. Possibly do it as a competitive activity, with SS working in teams to a time limit.

● **Exercise 4** To save time, give each pair a vowel sound and get them to write their examples on the board.

● **Exercise 5** Look at *Sounds English* and *Teaching English Pronunciation* (see *Bibliography*) for more on sound/spelling relationships.

## VOCABULARY

### Phrasal verbs

This is the first time that phrasal verbs have been practised, although they have come up earlier in vocabulary exercises (see Review Unit 4). Make it clear to SS that learning to use phrasal verbs has to be an on-going process, and that they should keep a list in their vocabulary books.

● **Exercise 1** Make it clear to SS that it is not always possible to work out the meaning of a phrasal verb from the verb and the particle/preposition, and that the meaning of *up* and *down* illustrated in the unit is not the only one. You could get SS to check their predictions in a dictionary.

SS are not yet required to decide where the adverb particle goes (that is dealt with in Unit 15). However, you might like to draw their attention to sentences b), c), and f) where the adverb particle has only one position because of the pronoun (see the *Language reference* in Unit 15). Show them how, for example, replacing *me* with *the girl* in sentence b) would mean that two positions are possible for the particle. Similarly you could substitute *them* for *your cigarettes* in sentence a) to demonstrate that only one position is possible. It is probably not worth going into the differences between adverb particles and prepositions here – there is more work on this area in Unit 15.

The WB has further exercises on phrasal verbs with *up* and *down*, and different phrasal verbs using *take*.

## SPEAKING

● **Exercise 1**   Obviously an open question. Might include ideas concerning the size of the brain as people become increasingly more intelligent.

● **Exercise 3**   SS could each be given a different topic to discuss in groups before presenting their ideas to the rest of the class. The main aim is oral fluency, although hopefully SS will also get a lot of practice in future forms.

## CREATIVE WRITING

● **Exercise 1**   This extract is quite dramatic – possibly read the extract aloud while SS listen or follow the text. You might like to get SS to try and guess what vocabulary such as *sunnyside up*, *rubbers*, *weather box*, etc. are.

● **Exercise 2**   An opportunity to introduce features of story writing (picked up later in Unit 18).

● **Exercises 3 and 4**   Give SS time to think individually and then let them share ideas in groups. One student could then write down the story and each member of the group check it.

# Tapescripts

### RECORDING 1

Well, I think houses in the future will probably be quite small but I should think they'll be well-insulated so that you don't need so much heating and cooling as you do now, so perhaps very economical to run. Perhaps they will use solar heating, although I don't know, in this country, perhaps we won't be able to do that so much. Yes, I think they'll be full of electronic gadgets: things like very advanced televisions, videos, perhaps videos which take up, the screen takes up the whole wall. I should think. Yes, you'll have things like garage doors which open automatically when you drive up, perhaps electronic sensors which will recognise you when you, when you come to the front door even. Perhaps architects and designers will be a bit more imaginative about how houses are designed and perhaps with the shortage of space people will think of putting gardens on the roof and, and maybe rooms can be expanded and, and contracted depending on what you use them for, so perhaps there'll be a bit more flexibility about that.

### RECORDING 2

girl, driver, sad, fall, knee, flu, drink, when, good, fun, wash, farm

# Key

### READING

### Before reading

**2**
a) Small.
b) Cheaper, because they will be well-insulated (maybe with solar heating).
c) Advanced televisions; videos where the screen takes up all the wall; garage doors which open automatically as you drive up; electronic sensors that recognise you when you get to the front door.
d) On the roof.
e) By expanding and contracting the size of the rooms.

### Reading

**1**
A video screen taking up a whole wall; a garage door opening automatically; a garden on the roof

**2**
The dome; lush plants; a 'power wall'; a glass roof

**3**
Predicted: a), d), e), g), h)
Not predicted: b), c), f)

**4**
a) gigantic   b) flit   c) fancy   d) oversee   e) chores
f) loft   g) loathe

**5**

Examples:

Imperative forms: *Imagine a house heated …*

Asking shortened direct questions: *And the washing?*

Use of impersonal *you*: *When you get bored …*

Missing words: *What, no electric sockets?*

Contracted forms: *He'll pay bills and order food …*

Exclamation marks: *There will be plenty of room for fun!*

## LANGUAGE POINT 1

### Time conjunctions

a) Your door will be opened *as soon as* it hears a voice it recognises.

You'll be able to see what your guests are wearing *before* they arrive.

*After* your guests leave make it smaller again.

Simply place it in the integrated laundry *until* it comes out ready to wear.

*When* you get bored, simulators will provide any experience.

b) The present tense (Present Simple or Continuous). It refers to the future.

## PRACTICE

**1**

a) until   b) before   c) when   d) after   e) as soon as

## LANGUAGE POINT 2

### *If* or *when*?

**1**

*If you're bored* means that there is a possibility that the person will be bored.

*When you're bored* means that it is certain that the person will be bored.

**2**

Correct: c) and e)

a) … if it doesn't rain.

b) When you wake up …

d) … when I grow up.

f) If you don't give me the money …

## LANGUAGE POINT 3

### Future Passive

a) No. No.   b) *will be filtered*

## PRACTICE

**1**

a) One of the conference organisers' representatives.

b) Complete the formalities, get information about the conference, and go on a sight-seeing tour.

c) We don't know.

**2**

a) You *will be met* in the arrivals hall …

… and *taken* by car to our headquarters.

There you *will be asked* to complete …

… and *will be given* the necessary papers …

… you *will* then *be taken* on a short sight-seeing tour …

… we *will be joined* by the Director General.

… a taxi *can be ordered* immediately …

b) The passive is often used in a semi-formal letter because it is less personal.

**3**

… you will be able to attend

… to complete the required formalities

… we will be joined by …

… to have your presence …

… We look forward to …

**4**

b) I'll show you to your room now.

c) The rain forests will be better protected in the future.

d) My parents will buy me a present if I pass.

e) At this stage the wine will be left for six months.

f) The army will not be given a pay rise this year.

g) Do you think you'll be offered the job?

h) We're holding a party tomorrow.

## PRONUNCIATION

### Vowels

**3**

driver /ə/; sad /æ/; fall /ɔː/; knee /iː/; flu /uː/; drink /ɪ/; when /e/; good /ʊ/; fun /ʌ/; wash /ɒ/; farm /ɑ/

**5**

a) taxi /'tæksi/

b) dinner /dɪnə/

c) necessary /'nesəsri/

d) tropical /'trɒpɪkəl/

e) border /'bɔːdə/

f) underneath /ʌndə'niːθ/

g) afternoon /ɑːftə'nuːn/

h) murder /'mɜːdə/

i) naughty /'nɔːti/

j) rocket /'rɒkɪt/

k) toothbrush /'tuːθbrʌʃ/

l) woollen /'wʊlən/

## VOCABULARY

### Phrasal verbs

**1**

1 h)  2 i)  3 g)  4 b)  5 f)  6 e)  7 a)  8 c)  9 d)

**2**

a) cut down   b) brought … up   c) cheer … up

d) hurry up   e) wind down   f) heat … up

g) slows … down   h) grows up   i) turn … down

## CREATIVE WRITING

**1**

a) A talking clock; a device which makes breakfast for all the family; something which says what you have to remember on that particular date; a weather box saying what the weather will be like; an automatic garage.

**2**

a) TWCSR   b) DSD   c) TWCSR   d) DSD

# Is the service good enough?

## Students' Book

**General theme**: services.
**Unit topic**: hotels and restaurants.

**SPEAKING**: choosing a hotel.
**LISTENING**: booking into a hotel.
**LANGUAGE POINT 1**: requests and offers.
**LANGUAGE POINT 2**: agreeing to / refusing requests.

**PRONUNCIATION**: using intonation (polite/impolite/sarcastic).
**READING**: newspaper interview with hotel manager.
**VOCABULARY**: hotels; verbs to nouns.

**SPEAKING**: discussion about service; roleplay: ordering a meal.
**WRITING**: notes and messages.

## Workbook

**LISTENING**: dialogues in different 'service' situations (e.g. optician's).
**FUNCTIONS**: requesting and asking permission; apologising and making excuses.
**VOCABULARY**: adjectives into nouns; cooking (simmer, etc., utensils).
**PRONUNCIATION**: short and long vowels; sound and spelling (vowel sounds / vowel letters).
**WRITING**: writing a dialogue between waiter and customer.

## Language

This unit is concerned with language 'functions' such as *making requests, agreeing/refusing* and *offers.*

## Common problems

### Request forms

As indicated in the *Language reference*, request forms can be a problem. There are many ways of making requests in English, and in British English the wordier the form the more polite it is (*I wonder if you'd mind ... ? / Do you think you could possibly ... ?* – i.e. tentative and indirect). However, the biggest problem for SS is intonation. Intonation determines whether we are acceptably polite (and get what we want) or unacceptably impolite and offend someone we have no wish to offend. Don't forget: most native speakers make allowances for SS' grammatical errors but are less prepared to make allowances for their intonational errors.

Most other languages except Dutch use intonation quite differently from English and SS' voice-range can often sound unacceptably restricted. This can be interpreted by the hearer as arrogance or boredom. Some SS can also sound very abrupt and rude to British ears. (It shouldn't be forgotten that British English intonation transferred to another language can sound equally peculiar.)

To be on the safe side, SS should be advised to say 'please' when they make requests (even in most informal contexts). Also, when they ask a stranger for something, they should start their request with their voice at a higher pitch (it can sound more tentative and respectful) and if possible finish on a slight rising tone. Try to show the flexibility of intonation and that it really affects what is being communicated. In the PRACTICE section on intonation, it's easier if SS can think themselves into the situation and act it out.

## Other problems

**1** The British sometimes use polite forms sarcastically or as a joke. This is touched on in the unit but don't spend too long on it or encourage practice – it is too subtle, dangerous and culture-specific at this level. It has been included for listening comprehension and to warn SS that when they use a very polite form in an inappropriate situation they might be misinterpreted!

**2** SS often leave out *will* when offering to do things: *\*I do that straightaway.*

# SPEAKING

● **Exercise 1**  Possibly start by revising some of the vocabulary from Unit 8 (e.g. *flat, furniture, caravan, houseboat,* etc.)

Get SS to discuss what they like and dislike about the different places in the photographs and elicit the vocabulary (e.g. *youth hostel* in the second photograph, and *bed and breakfast* or *B&B* in the fourth photograph). Compare the different kinds of hotel (the modern, international hotel in the first photograph and the traditional 'country-house' type in the third photograph). Ask what other places one can stay at: e.g. *guest in a family, 'pension'* – in some countries.

Be sensitive to SS who may not have stayed in luxurious hotels. Possibly modify the activity to get SS to compile a list of things they would want out of any hotel before they look at the list.

● **Exercise 2**  Get SS to help each other with the vocabulary of services. You may want to get hold of a hotel brochure and get SS to label the pictures. Another possibility is to match facilities with needs (e.g. ask questions like: *'What do you want if the weather is very hot? What do you ask for when your clothes are dirty?'*). The exercise also provides a good opportunity for revision of comparative forms.

# LISTENING

Purpose: to prepare for LANGUAGE POINT 1 (*Requests and offers*).

Lead into the situation (e.g. *'What does the receptionist ask when you book into a hotel?'*) and deal with possible problem words needed for the task: e.g. *reserve, book, car registration.*

● **Exercise 1**  Get SS to listen once to fill in the form. Possibly get them first to practise asking questions using the form (e.g. *'What is the registration number of your car?'*) and then to compare their question forms with the structures used in the dialogue.

● **Exercise 2**  Focuses on the language to be practised in LANGUAGE POINT 1. Stop tape so SS can write exact words or let SS listen to the target structures often enough to copy (in the language laboratory?). You might want SS to practise the intonation of the questions. Note the use of *will* (*'ll*) and the Present Continuous when talking about future personal arrangements (*'I'm coming back on the 21st.'*).

# LANGUAGE POINT 1

## Requests and offers

● **Exercise 1**  Check SS understand 'requests' (e.g. ask them to open the window) and 'offers' (e.g. someone is carrying a lot of books; say you'll carry some).

● **Exercise 2**  You may want to refer back to the work on less direct questions in Review Unit 1.

● **Exercise 3**  Focuses on form whereas Exercise 5 also shows the importance of intonation.

● **Exercise 5**  Extend by getting SS to practise (PW) and continue each exchange any way they like. Possibly also ask SS to reword the requests and make them polite or rude. Make sure they bring the dialogues to life and make them amusing.

# LANGUAGE POINT 2

## Agreeing to / Refusing requests

Ways of not agreeing include: *I'd like to but …; Sorry but …; I'm afraid I …* Extra work on intonation may be appropriate here. Other practice situations:
– A schoolfriend wants a lift home. You are going to the station to meet your brother.
– Your teacher wants you to read a whole book over the weekend. You have visitors at home.
– A traffic warden wants you to move your car. You have a puncture.

After this exercise direct SS to the exercise in the WB.

# PRONUNCIATION

## Using intonation

● **Exercise 3**   Make sure SS know what 'sarcastic' means (i.e. to use expressions which mean the opposite of what we feel in order to hurt). Try to do so by example rather than by explanation (e.g. ask someone to do something unpleasant like drop your books on the floor and say *How very kind of you!* using a sarcastic intonation).

● **Exercise 5**   See the *Language* notes above. Possibly let SS try these out first (PW), then elicit some models from the class, then more practice (PW) in which another student responds to each request.

Show SS the intonation of each request (using your hand?) e.g. the different pitch and voice range in a) and b); the flat tone in c).

# PRACTICE

● **Exercise 3**   Explain *humming* and *swearing*. Get SS A and B to take it in turns to make requests.

# READING

Point out that the Ritz is one of the smartest or 'poshest' hotels in London.

● **Exercise 1**   You might want to ask SS to use the title to predict what the article might be about. Difficult words (e.g. *comply, pastry, impress, conducive, deal, retain, invaluable, day off*) can be deduced from context before checking with the dictionary. Some SS may need to know that *Concorde* is an expensive/exclusive very fast plane to the USA and 'Phantom of the Opera' is a popular musical. Probably explain *rubber gloves*.

● **Exercise 2**   Checks comprehension (PW/GW?).

● **Exercise 3**   Could be done as a speaking rather than a writing activity. Connects with LANGUAGE POINTS 1 and 2. Possibly SS could think of other request situations and write or act out their dialogues.

# VOCABULARY

## Hotels

Can be used to revise the relative pronoun *who*.

Ask SS to guess word stress, check in the dictionary, and record words in their vocabulary books under the heading of a 'word-family' (e.g. *Hotels*).

## Verbs to nouns

Use dictionaries to check pronunciation and word stress. SS will need to practise the pronunciation of *-tion* (/ʃən/) and the weak pronunciation of *e* in *-ment* (/mənt/). There is another exercise on this in the WB.

# SPEAKING

● **Exercise 1**   Revision of 'giving advice'.

● **Exercises 2 and 3**   PW/GW. Aims to get SS to compare attitudes and raise awareness of socio-cultural differences (e.g. Does class or wealth make a difference?). Some examples here are not uncommon in some countries (e.g. in Japan, clapping twice). Other possibilities: shouting 'Waiter' or 'Listen'. Treat the activity lightly as 'fun'.

● **Exercise 4**   You will need to check the vocabulary first. Also (as a follow-up) compare this menu with a typical menu from SS' own country?

● **Exercise 5**   Give the 'waiter' and 'customers' time to prepare. The activity can be shortened or lengthened by taking away or adding to the constraints (e.g. specify that only two items are available for first and main course). Other possibilities: use other (real?) menus; use rolecards which make the situation more specific. Note the vocabulary of cooking (WB Unit 11) and the vocabulary of food (WB Unit 15).

# WRITING

## Notes and messages

● **Exercises 2 and 3**  Contrast semi-formal and personal tones (e.g. messages 1 and 2 in Exercise 2), though the difference is not so marked as in prose. Draw attention to punctuation features (see SB page 150).

# Tapescripts

## RECORDING 1

HOTEL RECEPTIONIST:  Mermaid, Luton. Can I help you?
GUEST:  Yes, I'd like to book a room for the night of the 14th, please.
HR:  Er, the 14th. … Yes, that's OK. Single, twin or double?
G:  Oh, double, please. With a bathroom. Could you tell me how much that'll cost?
HR:  Er, yes madam. That'll be £95, including breakfast. Can you give me your name, please?
G:  Yes, the name's Kate Andrews.
HR:  And your daytime telephone number?
G:  Yes, during the day … 0799 719377.
HR:  … 377. Thank you.
G:  Oh, another thing. Would it be possible to leave my car with you? I'm flying to Paris the next day and I'd like to leave it in your hotel car park.
HR:  Yes, certainly. How long for?
G:  A week. I'm coming back on the 21st.
HR:  OK. I'll reserve you a place for eight days. Would you give me the number and make of your car, please?
G:  Yes, it's a Golf and the registration number is H86 LYA. By the way, I don't suppose you could book me another room at the same time, could you? I want a double room for the night of the 21st.
HR:  The night of the 21st. … Yes, that's fine. What time will you be arriving on the 14th?
G:  I should think around 10 – 10 o'clock in the evening.
HR:  In the evening? Shall I order you a late dinner?
G:  If you would, yes.
HR:  OK. Well, if you could confirm this in writing, please.
G:  Yes, I'll do that now. Thank you very much. Goodbye.
HR:  Thank you madam. Goodbye.

## RECORDING 2

a)  A: Could I have some ice, please?
   B: Yes, of course. I'll send some up at once.
b)  A: Would you mind sending champagne and chips to my room at 4 a.m., please?
   B: I'll try, sir, but on Wednesdays the kitchen staff leave at midnight.
c)  A: Can you show me to my room, please?
   B: Certainly, sir.

d)  A: I'm terribly sorry, sir, but would you mind not smoking in the foyer, please? It's one of our rules.
   B: Oh, of course not. I didn't realise.
e)  A: I was wondering if I could borrow a dressing gown.
   B: No, madam, I'm afraid we don't lend items of clothing. There's a big department store next door. They might be able to help you.

## RECORDING 3

a)  MAN:  I don't suppose I can give you a lift home, can I?
   WOMAN: Oh, clear off! You're getting on my nerves.

b)  WOMAN:  I want to try on that black pair.
   SHOP ASSISTANT:  Oh! I thought the red ones looked very nice on you.

c)  BARMAN:  What would you like madam?
   CUSTOMER:  Oh, just a half. Do you sell food?

d)  FATHER:  I don't suppose you could possibly turn that television off, could you?
   SON:  Sorry, Dad. I just want to watch this programme.

## RECORDING 4

1  'Sorry to bother you, Jim. It's Bob. I've got a problem. The car's broken down and I've got to get to London on Friday. I was wondering whether you could lend me yours for the day. Give me a ring and let me know, can you?'

2  'Oh, Gill. I'm sorry you're out. I don't like answerphones. It's Sally. I'm really thrilled about the news. Ray, Ray told me this morning. When is it? We are going to get an invite, aren't we? Listen, I'll, I'll phone you next week. All right? See you.'

3  'Hello, this is Mrs Wong from Cyberpic International. I know you're closed now but I wondered if you could get a message through to Mr Miller, the Managing Director, first thing in the morning. Could you tell him I was expecting someone to meet me at Sydney Airport and take me to my hotel? As I don't know where your offices are he'll have to contact me at the Hilton. Thank you.'

4  'Hi, Dave. This is your old pal, Frank. Remember? I heard your sister was ill. Mavis. I used to go out with her once. Lovely woman. You couldn't let me have her phone number, could you? I want to get in touch with her again. You know, to see if I could help. OK? Cheers.'

# Key

## LISTENING

**1**

Name: *Kate Andrews*
Phone number: *0799 719377*
Type of room requested: *Double, with a bathroom*
Dates: *14th*
Special requests: *Wants to leave car for eight days.*
Car registration: *H86 LYA*
Time of arrival: *10 p.m.*

**2**

a) Could you tell me …
b) Can you give me …
c) Would it be possible …
d) I'll …
e) Would you give me …
f) I don't suppose you could …
g) I'll do that …

## LANGUAGE POINT 1

### Requests and offers

**1**

i) a), b), c), e), f)
ii) d) and g)

**2**

c) and f)

**3**

Most polite: b), d)    Least polite: a), c)

**5**

d) and e)

## LANGUAGE POINT 2

### Agreeing to / Refusing requests

**1**

a) Yes, of course. I'll … (*agree*)
b) I'll try but … (*not agree?*)
c) Certainly. (*agree*)
d) Of course not. I … (*agree*)
e) No, I'm afraid … (*not agree*)

## PRONUNCIATION

### Using intonation

**1**

a) 4   b) 1   c) 3   d) 2

**2**

a) A young man at a party is trying to give a young girl a lift home.
b) A woman is trying on different colour shoes.
c) A woman is asking a barman for half a pint of beer and asking if they sell food.
d) A father is trying to get his son to turn off the television.

**3**

a) Man trying to be polite; woman impolite.
b) Customer rude; assistant quite polite.
c) Barman and customer: both polite.
d) Father is sarcastic (falsely polite).

**4**

The barman's voice (dialogue b) starts at a high pitch because he is addressing a stranger for the first time and he wants to be polite.

## PRACTICE

**1**

Formality depends on the relationship and how distant/formal the speakers want to be. Items 1 and 3 are more likely to be formal because they are formal situations (but in reality people are often neither formal nor polite in these situations). In item 4 it depends on the greengrocer; in item 2 it depends on whether the lecturer knows the young student or not. In all these situations people could use polite forms to be sarcastic.

Examples:
2  'What do you think you're doing? Put that newspaper down!'
3  'Excuse me, sir. Do you think you could put your feet down? Somebody's got to sit there later.'
4  'Excuse me, madam. Would you mind not touching the fruit?'

**2**

Examples:
a) 'I'd like to increase my overdraft. Would that be possible?'
b) 'Excuse me. Could you tell me the way to the post office, please?'
c) 'Sorry to trouble you, but do you think I could possibly leave early today?'

## READING

**2**

a) … whatever they want without sounding surprised.
b) … the manager to marry him and his fiancée.
c) … he wanted his girlfriend to marry him.
d) … use top hotels as a place for getting someone to agree to something.
e) … he wanted him to pretend he knew him when he came in with two other men.
f) … they have good contacts.

**3**

Examples:
a) 'Do you think I could possibly borrow some rubber gloves?'
b) 'I wonder if you'd mind marrying me and my fiancée.'
c) 'Could you put this ring in the strawberry tart?'
d) 'I wonder if you'd mind saying "Good morning, Mr Smith" when I walk through the door.'
e) 'Excuse me, do you know any way I could get a ticket for *Phantom of the Opera*?'

## VOCABULARY

### Hotels

b) Someone who watches the door, lets people in and out and helps people find taxis.

c) Someone who deals with guests on arrival.

d) Someone who cleans and tidies bedrooms.

e) Someone (who is) in charge of money and payments.

f) Someone who makes telephone connections at a switchboard.

Others: e.g. general manager, catering manager, cook, chef, cleaner, page, commissionaire, etc.

### Verbs to nouns

**1**

a) explanation  b) discussion  c) hesitation
d) decision  e) enjoyment  f) embarrassment

**2**

a) choice  b) complaint  c) arrival  d) success
e) failure  f) appearance  g) behaviour

## WRITING

### Notes and messages

**1**

a) By underlining or by putting them in capitals.

b) *I have a* table booked for 8 *o'clock. I have* taken *the* car to *the* mechanic. *It's* still making a funny noise. *I'll be* back before 6 *o'clock*. Please feed *the* cat. *There is a* tin open in *the* fridge.

c) Dashes and exclamation marks. (Also dots and question marks.)

**2**

*Message 1*

a) Possibly Helen is a secretary to her boss, Philip. She is telling him to return an urgent call.

b) Semi-formal situation. A full formal form would be 'Would you be able to phone him back … ?'

*Message 2*

a) Angry and frustrated husband/wife/friend. Wants to say that he/she has wasted the meal that the other person didn't turn up for and has given it to the dog.

b) Very personal. Notice the highly abbreviated and humorous/rude tone and personal use of question marks.

*Message 3*

a) A neighbour wanting to complain about Judy parking her car too close so that she can't get out.

b) Semi-informal: they are using first names and informal terms like 'thanks' but Rachel uses the polite form 'Would you mind not … ?' rather sharply.

*Message 4*

a) A flatmate asking the other flat mate to pay the milkman.

b) Informal and relaxed use of the direct imperative: 'Don't forget … '

*Message 5*

a) A boy/girlfriend is making an appointment to meet at the Pizza Express restaurant.

b) The very personal 'Darling', the use of !!! and the imperative ('Don't …') show that it is very informal.

**3**

*Message 1*

Jim,
Car broken down – got to get to London on Friday. OK if I borrow yours for the day? Give me a ring.
Bob

*Message 2*

Gill,
Ray told me the news this morning. Very exciting. Are we going to get an invite? Will phone next week.
See you,
Sally

*Message 3*

Mr Miller,
Was expecting to be met at Sydney Airport. Don't know where your offices are. Contact me at the Hilton.
Mrs Wong

*Message 4*

Dave,
Heard Mavis was ill. Want to get in touch. Want to help. Could you let me have her phone no.? Still working at pub.
Cheers,
Frank

# Money, money, money

## Students' Book

**General theme:** services.
**Unit topic:** spending money.

**LISTENING:** lead-in newspaper article about an old lady who left £500,000 when she died; songs about money.
**VOCABULARY 1:** money expressions.

**LANGUAGE POINT 1:** imaginary situations – the second conditional.
**LANGUAGE POINT 2:** *wish* + past tense, to express dissatisfaction.
**VOCABULARY 2:** theft.

**SPEAKING:** discussion on moral issues about stealing.
**CREATIVE WRITING:** magazine article about 'shopaholics', leading to group letter writing.

## Workbook

**READING:** magazine article about how manufacturers get customers to buy products.
**GRAMMAR:** the second conditional; conditionals and *wish*; prepositional phrases.
**VOCABULARY:** buying.
**PRONUNCIATION:** vowel sounds.
**WRITING:** dictation.

## Language

This unit's language focus is on imaginary or impossible situations in the present and future, and the structures practised are the second conditional and *wish* + the past. Also revised in this unit are *could* for ability and ways of giving advice.

The first conditional, introduced in Unit 9, is revised and contrasted with the second conditional.

## Common problems
### Second conditional

**1**   SS often make mistakes with which tenses to use in the two clauses, and get them mixed up. In German, for example, *would* is used in both clauses. In some languages (e.g. Turkish), the third conditional can be used for an impossible condition in the present. On the other hand, Arabic has no third conditional and instead uses the second conditional with time adverbs.

There is often confusion between the form of the first and second conditional (*If I would have a lot of money I will go.*).

**2**   Whether to use the 'first' or the 'second' conditional depends on how the situation is seen (i.e. if it is possible or impossible/improbable). SS often find this very difficult to grasp.

**3**   Point out that *were* is often used instead of *was* after *if*, and especially in formal situations.

**4**   SS need a lot of practice in recognising contracted forms and weak forms in the conditional (*If I were* (/wə/) *you, I'd* (/aɪd/) *leave home.*) as well as lots of practice in producing it.

**5**   It may well be that SS will come across other variations from the norm for the first and second conditional (e.g. *If I saw him he always smiled.*), so point out that there are exceptions.

### Wish + past tense

**1** The main problem here is the idea of an unreal situation in the present or future expressed with a past tense. This is similar to the second conditional, so the second conditional and *wish* are probably best taught together. *Wish* equals *if only* for most West Europeans. For some nationalities it helps to explain that the use of the past acts like a subjunctive.

**2** The difference between *wish* + past and *wish* + *would* (to express annoying habits, and a hope for change in the future) has not been introduced in this unit to avoid confusion (see *Upper Intermediate Matters*).

**3** Point out that *wish* can be followed by either *was* or *were*.

# LISTENING

## Before listening

● **Exercise 1** Useful vocabulary: *to get into debt, convenient, live on credit, pay high interest*. This activity links up well with the reading text later in the CREATIVE WRITING section.

● **Exercise 2** Useful words to elicit/teach connected to the lexical area of money would be: *jumble sales, bargain, extravagant, gamble, spend/win money on*. Make sure that SS realise that the old lady left £500,000 in her will (i.e. she was very rich!). Possibly discuss what 'useful things' she might have found on the beach, and other ways of gambling, apart from fruit machines.

● **Exercise 4** The quiz is partly for fun and to get SS speaking to each other (and should be approached in this way in case any SS take it too personally!). It could be done as PW/GW or let the class mingle. Alternatively, it could be done with other SS in the school, or with native speakers, if possible. However, it also introduces some more vocabulary connected with money, which will come up again later in the unit, and it will probably be necessary to go over this before SS do the quiz. Vocabulary to highlight could include: *cash, go shopping, purse/wallet, waste money, owe, pay off, overdraw/overdraft*.

Encourage SS to make a note of new *Money* vocabulary in their notebooks. You may prefer at this point to 'jump' directly to the VOCABULARY section and/or include the exercise in the WB.

## Listening

You may want to tell SS that the first song is by ABBA, the Swedish pop group and the second song is from the musical *Fiddler on the Roof*.

● **Exercises 1 and 2** The aim of the first recording (*Money, Money, Money*) is listening comprehension. The second recording introduces the idea of an imaginary situation (*If I Were a Rich Man*) and the second conditional. Possibly go on directly from this to LANGUAGE POINT 1 (*Imaginary situations*).

An alternative approach is to give one group one song and the other group the other song and then exchange answers and views about it. This could be done in the language laboratory.

Other songs around the same topic could be included here, such as the Beatles' *(Money) Can't Buy Me Love* and *Money Makes The World Go Round* from the musical, *Cabaret*.

# VOCABULARY 1

## Money expressions

Some of this language (*spend money on, bargain, overdrawn, owe*) is revision of vocabulary which has already come up in the unit; other new words can be deduced from the context. This activity could be preceded by a 'brainstorm' in which SS write down as many words or expressions as they know connected to money, and share the vocabulary in groups.

SS could be asked to check the pronunciation (sounds and word stress) of the words in a dictionary. The weak vowels (emboldened) in *a**ff**ord, ove**r**drawn* and *barg**ai**n* could be pointed out.

An extra vocabulary activity could be idiomatic words or expressions connected to money, e.g. *made of money, money doesn't grow on trees, money burns a hole in my pocket*, etc.

# LANGUAGE POINT 1

## Imaginary situations

● **Exercise 1** The aim of the listening is for the SS to hear examples of the second conditional in a natural context, but not to focus on the grammar yet. Don't worry if SS make grammatical mistakes in giving you the answers – it is enough that they understand the meaning of the structure. Possibly begin by eliciting from SS different things they or other people would spend a lot of money on if they suddenly won it (possibly showing picture cues to give ideas). In this way you can introduce the vocabulary needed for the listening extracts, such as *business* and *luxurious hotel*. You could also get SS to predict from the cues what the people interviewed are going to say and then get them to listen to check their predictions.

● **Exercises 3 and 4**   Write the two example sentences (*If I had all the money that I wanted, I'd give up my job.* and *If I were you, I'd look for a new job.*) on the board and then get SS to repeat them. Practise the clauses separately at first, using correct sentence stress, the weak form of *was* and *were*, and the contracted form – *I'd*. Note that *would* and *were* in the question are also weak (*What would* /wəd/ *you do if you were* /wə/ *me?*). Highlight the forms of the verbs and emphasise that the two clauses can change places in the sentence. Explain that *If I **was** you* is also possible, but that *were* is used more often.

● **Exercise 5**   This contrasts the first and second conditional and so provides revision of work done in Unit 9. Focus on both form and use. Use the pictures to elicit example sentences.

● **Exercise 6**   Shows how flexible the structure can be, e.g. the past tense can be replaced by the Past Continuous, and *would* can be replaced by *might/could*, just as *will* can be replaced by *may*, *might*, and *could*. It also highlights common errors.

## PRACTICE

● **Exercise 1**   An important exercise because it forces SS to think about the area of possibility or improbability which influences their choice of conditional sentence.

● **Exercise 2**   This is a personalised exercise, as is Exercise 4, and could be done in pairs or groups. See also *Grammar Practice Activities* and *Grammar in Action* (see *Bibliography*) for other communication activities practising conditional forms.

● **Exercise 3**   Gives practice in manipulating the construction. There is more work in the WB.

## LANGUAGE POINT 2

### Wish

● **Exercise 1**   Possibly personalise by giving a situation relevant to SS, e.g. *Saeed is always late. I wish he wasn't/weren't, but he always is.* Or use pictures of situations (e.g. a dark rainy day) and ask the SS questions to establish the situation (*'What kind of day is it?'*) before giving further examples (*'I wish it were warm and sunny.'*).

● **Exercise 2**   Make it clear that *would* could be used in place of *could*.

● **Exercise 3**   These sentences could be expanded to give extra practice in the second conditional. Example:
*I wish it were Friday because I am not at work the next day.*
*I wish it were Friday because if it were I wouldn't have to work the next day.*

## VOCABULARY 2

### Theft

Possibly get SS to make 'word family' charts (for words like *steal, rob, burgle, mug*, etc.) in their vocabulary books, with different columns for the noun, verb and person. Get them to use their dictionaries to check the words. This vocabulary is useful for the following SPEAKING activity.

## SPEAKING

The aim of these activities is to get SS to discuss their opinions, using some of the vocabulary studied in the previous section. For extra oral practice you could develop it into a mini-roleplay with three students taking the parts of Andrew, Tina and Janet, and somebody interviewing them.

● **Exercise 1, c)**   There is more work in Unit 13 on looking up colloquial language in the dictionary. Possibly begin looking up colloquial expressions now if appropriate. You may also want to highlight phrasal verbs such as *get away with, knock down, run off* and *bring up*.

# CREATIVE WRITING

● **Exercise 1**  Could be developed into a roleplay, e.g. an interview with the 'shopaholic'. Otherwise use it as a lead-in discussion to the writing. But be sensitive to SS who may have suffered from this themselves, or who may be quite poor and not feel that this is relevant to them.

● **Exercise 2**  Ties in with the *Before listening* at the beginning of the unit, where SS were asked to think of the problems of having credit cards. Vocabulary which SS have met in this or previous units: *obsession, debts, cheer up, credit, symptoms*. Although not a text intended to be looked at intensively, possibly highlight vocabulary such as: *splash out, increase, crack down, withdraw*.

Item a) could be done for homework, if you have no time in class, but group letter writing can be an interesting and useful activity from time to time.

In item c) focus on intonation when giving advice.

# Tapescripts

## RECORDING 1

I work all night I work all day
To pay the bills I have to pay
Ain't it sad!
And still there never seems to be
A single penny left for me
That's too bad!
In my dreams I have a plan
If I got me a wealthy man
I wouldn't have to work at all
I'd fool around and have a ball

Money, money, money
Must be funny
In the rich man's world
Money, money, money
Always sunny
In the rich man's world
Aha, aha, all the things I could do
If I had a little money
It's a rich man's world …

## RECORDING 2

If I were a rich man
Diddle deedle diddle digga digga deedle diddle dum
All day long I'd iddy biddy bum
If I were a wealthy man
Wouldn't have to work hard
Diddle deedle diddle digga digga deedle diddle dum
If I were an iddy biddy rich
Iddle diddle diddle deedle man

I'd build a big tall house
With rooms by the dozen
Right in the middle of the town
A fine tin roof with real wooden floors below
There could be one long staircase just going up
And one even longer coming down
And one more leading nowhere just for show

## RECORDING 3

KEITH:  Well, actually I think probably the first thing I'd do because I've got a bit of a weakness for nice cars – I love Mercedes Benz cars – there's something about really nice … I think I'd waste a bit of money on a nice car …

SUE:  I think, I think I would want to perhaps do something completely different with my life. I think I might actually give up my job and go back to college and perhaps study medicine and try to become a doctor.

BEN:  If I had all the money I wanted and was going to spend it on myself then I would travel in great comfort. I think that would be one of the main things. I, I love travelling. Nowadays it is expensive to travel in comfort. I read travel magazines. I read about all sorts of luxurious hotels in other parts of the world and I think, well, I would like to go and spend two weeks in the Bel-Air hotel in Los Angeles and that's what I'd spend my money on if it was for me.

NORMA:  I would set my husband up in business back in Liverpool. He's a carpenter. And to go home, that's, that's all I want. But it's not possible now because there's no chance that he would get any work there. That would be lovely, wouldn't it?

# Key

## LISTENING

### Before listening

**2**

a) She ate very cheap food, bought second-hand clothes from jumble sales, looked for things on the beach, gambled on fruit machines and had a cooker which didn't work properly, and yet she was very rich.

b) Open answer. She hated spending money, perhaps.

**4**

Someone addicted to shopping.

### Listening

**1**

a) Yes.

b) Poor.

c) Marry a wealthy man. So that she wouldn't have to work.

d) A rich man's world.

**2**

a) No.

b) Work hard.

c) A big tall house.

d) In the middle of the town.

## VOCABULARY 1

### Money expressions

a) broke

b) overdrawn

c) bargain

d) wealthy

e) lends

f) afford

g) owe

h) on

i) earns

j) cost

## LANGUAGE POINT 1

### Imaginary situations

**1**

Sue would give up her job and study to be a doctor.
Ben would travel in great comfort and stay in luxurious hotels.
Norma would set her husband up in business, in Liverpool.

**3**

a) Present. b) Imaginary.

**4**

a) Present. b) Imaginary. c) Past tense (*were*).

**5**

a) First sentence. b) Second sentence.

**6**

a) and e)

## PRACTICE

**3**

a) were/was

b) would be able to

c) stopped

d) were

e) would take

## LANGUAGE POINT 2

### *Wish*

**1**

a) 1 I wish *I had* a car.

  2 I wish *I didn't* work here.

  3 I wish *I were* on a beach.

b) Past Simple or Past Continuous.

**2**

1 I wish I had a car because if I did I wouldn't need to wait in the cold for buses.

2 I wish I didn't work here because if I didn't I wouldn't be so bored.

3 I wish I were on a beach because if I were I'd be warm.

## VOCABULARY 2

### Theft

**1**

a) robbery

b) pickpocket

c) burglary

d) mugging

**2**

a) a burglar

b) a robber

c) a mugger

d) a thief

## SPEAKING

**1**

c) pinch, nick

# Layabout

## Students' Book

**General theme:** leisure.
**Unit topic:** eccentric people.

**READING:** article from popular newspaper about John Richards, a 'super slob'.
**VOCABULARY 1:** colloquial language (slang).
**VOCABULARY 2:** looking up idiomatic expressions in the dictionary.

**LANGUAGE POINT 1:** Present Perfect with *since/for* (unfinished past).
**LANGUAGE POINT 2:** Present Perfect Continuous (unfinished past).

**PRONUNCIATION:** sentence stress.
**SPEAKING:** preparing a radio news broadcast ('popular' versus 'serious').
**WRITING:** writing a summary of the news broadcast.

## Workbook

**LISTENING:** people talking about their dreams.
**GRAMMAR:** *since* or *for*?; writing questions with *How long ... ?*; Present Perfect Simple or Continuous; Present Simple/Continuous or Present Perfect Simple/Continuous.
**VOCABULARY:** idiomatic expressions – pairs (e.g. *here and there*).
**WRITING:** summary writing.

## Language

This unit focuses on the use of the Present Perfect Simple and the Present Perfect Continuous to refer to something which began in the past and has continued to the present (a related use to talk about 'result' in the present is focused on to a greater extent in *Upper Intermediate Matters*). For this 'unfinished past' use we need to refer to a period of time, usually using a phrase beginning *for* or *since*. To ask about a length of time we use the question phrase *How long* + Present Perfect. (This can be compared with *How long ago* + Past Simple.)

Remember the Present Perfect always refers to the past from a present perspective (see also Review Unit 4). Most languages express this 'concept' using a Present Simple form: *\*How long are you here? I am here for two years.*

## Common problems
### Present Perfect

**1**  *For* and *since* are often confused: *\*I have studied English since two years.*

**2**  The distinction between the Present Perfect Simple and the Present Perfect Continuous (both are 'aspects' not tenses) can be problematic. In some languages (e.g. Dutch) there are no continuous forms. In English the Present Perfect Continuous is used to focus on an event in progress (i.e. the activity itself) up to the present. Also see the *Language reference* in this unit and Review Unit 2 for the rule about stative verbs in relation to continuous forms. (Possibly use this unit to do some revision on this area.)

### Sentence stress

This unit also practises sentence stress. SS whose first language is syllable-timed (e.g. Brazilian Portuguese, West African languages, Thai, Greek) find it difficult to recognise (and use) a system of stress that helps the speaker convey meaning. Even SS from stress-timed languages (e.g. German) have problems with the 'weak forms' that are so much a part of the system of stress in English (see Review Units 1 and 3 and Unit 5).

# READING

## Before reading

The aim is to develop awareness of the differences between the style of 'serious' and 'popular' newspapers and prepare SS for the extreme form of 'popular' story in the *Reading*.

Possibly expand activity by bringing in English newspapers (if available) and SS' own newspapers and compare different versions of the same story.

Names of some British newspapers: *Guardian, The Observer, The Times, The Independent, The Daily Telegraph* ('serious'); *Daily Mail, Daily Express, Today* (more 'popular'); *Daily Mirror, Sun, Star, Sunday Sport* ('popular'). In Britain possibly tell SS the type of people each newspaper appeals to and the approximate circulation. Possibly, ask SS to classify any newspapers they know according to whether they are 'popular' or 'serious'.

Get SS (PW/GW) to make up a story (orally) behind one or two of the headlines?

Other headlines for practice: *Golfer killed by lightning; Elvis is alive and well; World faces ecological catastrophe; Mum abandoned baby in Marks and Spencer's bag; US research shows capitalism works; Di has secret lover.* (e.g. Which is the most/least 'serious'? Give reasons.)

Follow-up questions for 'popular' newspapers: Why are the headlines so big? (*They aim to catch the readers' attention.*); What sorts of stories are chosen? (*Gossipy, scandalous, sensationalist – half-truths only.*); What kind of pictures are used? (*Large, emotional, sensational.*); What kind of language is used? (*Informal, slangy, emotional.*).

## Reading

The text is from a 'tabloid' newspaper, the *Sunday Sport*, and may be fact or fiction – it is difficult to tell. It is nevertheless presented as fact, although written in a lurid, tongue-in-cheek ('over the top') style that's close to parody. (An attempt to get behind texts of this sort is made in Exercises 3 and 4 – possibly *optional.*)

The text is useful as an introduction to one type of text common in the English-speaking world, to colloquial language (particularly slang) and as a springboard for the Present Perfect Simple/Continuous with *since* and *for*. However, this text needs more preparation than usual before teaching.

● **Exercise 1**  Use to get SS to focus on gist at this stage and steer clear of detail and the (many) new colloquial/slangy words. Possibly get SS simply to underline important facts in case they feel the text is 'too difficult'.

Men first landed on the moon in 1969; the 'world war' was 1939–1945. The words 'I'm going upstairs – I may be some time.' in paragraph 2 seem to parody Captain Oates, the explorer on Captain Scott's Antarctic expedition in 1910, who, fearing he would be a hindrance to his colleagues, deliberately left his tent to die ('I'm going outside …').

Play down or ignore slang that a dictionary may not be much help with (e.g. *whacked-out wimp* which means a 'weak and exhausted useless man').

Many of the 'new' words are for recognition only. Some are dealt with in VOCABULARY 1; others are ignored (e.g. *munch, bug-infested, larder, goodies, candy, wrappers*, etc.). Explain only if necessary.

Note that the text's aim is to insult, laugh at and pretend to be shocked by this man (see Exercise 3).

● **Exercise 4**  Note also other techniques of sensationalism, e.g. capital letters (*SUPER SLOB*), punctuation (*an incredible 56 years!*).

Although linguistically difficult, the content usually provokes a strong reaction (comic with universal appeal, or offensive?) – dealt with in Exercise 5.

The WB LISTENING is about dreams. To link the John Richards text with the WB get SS to compile a questionnaire about sleeping habits (e.g. *When do you usually go to bed? How many hours do you sleep? What do you dream about? What do you do when you can't sleep? What do you wear in bed? What bedtime habits have you got?* etc.). Then PW/GW (to interview each other) or interview native speakers and compile a statistics chart.

# VOCABULARY 1

## Colloquial language

● **Exercise 1**  Possibly ask them which words *sound* the rudest (exaggerate your intonation?).

● **Exercise 2**  See *Reading* above. Put headings on the board, do one or two with the SS using dictionaries (check the words are there first!). Get

SS to notice which are marked as *slang* or *informal*. Resist practice of the new words. The aim is recognition rather than production. Warn SS that inappropriate use could cause them problems.

# VOCABULARY 2

## Looking up idiomatic expressions

● **Exercise 2** Advise SS not to (over-)use some of these expressions (e.g. b) ii) and vii) – they can easily sound odd. The aim is more recognition.

# LANGUAGE POINT 1

## Unfinished past: *since/for*

Possibly do some revision of the Present Perfect to talk about experience (see Review Unit 4) to help show common link with 'unfinished past' use (i.e. they both look at the past from the point of view of the present). Focus on the difference with the Past Simple (e.g. *How long* + Present Perfect versus *How long ago* + Past Simple). Put 'time-lines' on the board? (There is a further exercise in the WB.)

# LANGUAGE POINT 2

## Present Perfect Continuous

Remind SS which verbs don't take the continuous.

Discuss examples in the PRACTICE to get over the 'concept' of the Perfect Continuous aspect in contrast to the Perfect Simple aspect.

An alternative or extra roleplay is to focus on *How long ... ?* and the contrast between Present Perfect and Past Simple, e.g. doctor/patient situation:

DOCTOR: needs to know name; age; present address / length of time resident; previous address / length of time resident; illnesses suffered; present complaint, etc.

PATIENT: moved to Birmingham five months ago from Bristol (there five years); had measles, bronchitis, migraine, a mild heart attack two years ago; at the moment has a high temperature, headache, sickness and a cold.

(A job interview is another good situation.)

# PRONUNCIATION

## Sentence stress

● **Exercises 1–3** Aim to help SS identify content words; Exercises 4 and 5 focus on the stressed content word(s) in a sentence.

● **Exercise 4** Get SS to predict answers based on Exercises 1–3. (Decide on a system for marking sentence stress, possibly a box over the main stress in a word, and be consistent.) They could then read the sentences to themselves in the 'normal' way to see if they sound natural. Possibly practise weak forms of unstressed words (see WB Unit 14 and information on the *schwa* in SB Unit 6).

# SPEAKING

● **Exercise 1** Ask SS about similarities between 'serious' and 'popular' radio programmes and newspapers (e.g. in Britain, between the 'serious' BBC radio programme *Today* and the newspaper *The Independent*).

Possible questions to focus on radio broadcasts:
PROGRAMME 1: *What has happened to the cost of living? Why was it a surprise? What do we know about Prince Charles and Status Quo?*
PROGRAMME 2: *What has happened in Europe? What has happened on the railways?*

● **Exercise 2** As the focus is on speaking, possibly simply explain difficult vocabulary (e.g. *timewarp, stumble, spinster, PC, bluff, notable, twit*, etc.) or perhaps allocate different words to different SS to look up and explain. (Use the abbreviation *PC* to draw SS' attention to how abbreviations are dealt with in their dictionaries.)

If you have the resources, get SS to record their broadcast. If you have got video-filming equipment, turn the broadcast into a TV programme. Whether audio or video is used, rehearsals can be recorded, followed by GW discussion about improvements that could be made. Possible follow up: get SS to do different interviews with the same person, both informal and semi-formal.

# WRITING

## Summary writing

Notice that the main emphasis is on process rather than product (i.e. the drafting phase is given a lot of attention).

SS might need help sorting out factual prose from emotional/opinionated prose. Possibly, start one summary off on the board for other groups to see.

# Tapescripts

## RECORDING 1

a) I'm arriving at Heathrow on the 10 p.m. flight. Can you meet me, please?
b) There has been a new spy scandal and a minister has resigned.
c) Your father is very ill. You must return immediately.
d) We're having a wonderful time. The weather has been amazing. We've visited Niagara Falls and we're visiting Hollywood on Tuesday.
e) A famous actor has been arrested after his wife was found dead.

## RECORDING 2

a) He was walking down the street.
b) I'm going to the cinema with her.
c) She was holding a red coat.
d) Why don't you try taking two aspirin later?
e) She's got a very strong personality, hasn't she?

## RECORDING 3

### Programme 1

BEVERLY ROBERTS: At one o'clock. Inflation is at its highest level for eight years. Prince Charles comes out of hospital, the operation on his arm a success. His nurses say: 'He was an absolute sweetie.' And Status Quo tell us their plans for a major comeback. Beverly Roberts reporting.
  Trouble again for the Government. Prices have increased by over 10% for the first time since 1982. The new official statistics from the Government are a shock. They were expecting a rise in prices but not one of a full percentage point to 10.6%. Geoffrey Daniels has the details.
GEOFFREY DANIELS: There's no doubt that this is a disaster for the Government. I think everyone was saying that inflation would pass 10% but the worst forecast I heard in the City was 10.3%, so for it to leap up to 10.6% is very serious, and some would say shows the failure of the Government's present policies.
BEVERLY ROBERTS: Have you seen any Government ministers looking sheepish?
GEOFFREY DANIELS: I haven't seen any yet, but it's early days yet.

### Programme 2

ALAN TAYLOR: *The World Today*. Thirty minutes of news and comment. This is Alan Taylor. The headlines. The United Nations act together to secure world peace. We speak to the Secretary General about the Security Council's latest peace plan for Europe and we'll be seeking the views of the American Ambassador who explains why his country has its doubts. The Manchester Rail Disaster. We hear from British Rail and from those families fighting for compensation. And inflation is in double figures for the first time for eight years. In the twelve months to August, the Retail Price Index rose to 10.6%, much higher than expected. The Chancellor of the Exchequer tells *The World Today* that the figure will not change Government policy. The news now from Katherine Shepherd.
KATHERINE SHEPHERD: The Secretary General of the United Nations, Mr José Ricardo, has confirmed that the Security Council has agreed on a peace plan for Europe which it hopes …

# Key

## READING

### Before reading

**1**
A: a), d), e)     B: b), c)

### Reading

**1**
*World's laziest slob – hasn't been up since 1932*
a) 4   b) 1   c) 3   d) 5   e) 2

**2**
a) … thanks to the farm his parents left to him …
b) … John's devoted sister, Bessie …
c) … even she puts on rubber gloves, a plastic apron and wellies …
d) … but at least it's easy …

**3**
a) ii)   b) ii)   c) ii

**4**
a) True   b) True   c) False

The article is typical of the 'popular' tabloid press: it magnifies a trivial event, it is gossipy, humorous and unpleasant at the same time.

## VOCABULARY 1

### Colloquial language

**1**
layabout, lazybones, wimp

**2**
*Sleep*: kip, doze, snore, worn-out, turn in, cat-nap
*Laziness*: bone-idle, slob, layabout, lazybones
*Dirt*: grimy, sticky, mouldy

**3**
In particular: grimy, slob, layabout, mouldy

## VOCABULARY 2
### Looking up idiomatic expressions

**1**
finger

**2**
b) Examples:
   i) … I saw a boy steal some sweets in a shop.
   ii) … he explained the problem.
   iii) … she bites her nails.
   iv) … petrol. We'll have to walk.
   v) … told your father about your new girlfriend.
   vi) … could you lend me a couple of pounds?
   vii) … 's got all the answers right.
   viii) … come to the gym today.
   ix) … anybody to know about it.
   x) … to stop going out with him.
c)
   i) Pretend not to see
   ii) Be exactly right
   iii) Annoys someone very much (gets on someone's nerves)
   iv) Have no more (come to the end of)
   v) Say something wrong (make a boob)
   vi) Not have enough money (be broke)
   vii) Be able to think quickly
   viii) Be hurting
   ix) Keep something secret
   x) Be unreliable

## LANGUAGE POINT 1
### Unfinished past: *since/for*

**1**
*John hasn't sat up* **since** *1942.*
a) In 1942.
b) Yes.
c) For 46 years.(The article was written in 1988, so 1988 – 1942 = 46.)

*He's stayed in bed* **for** *56 years.*
a) Yes.
b) 56 years ago.
c) 56 years.

**2**
a) since  b) for  c) How long

## PRACTICE

a) He has had a beard for two years.
b) I haven't eaten seafood since I had food poisoning two months ago.
c) He hasn't got out of bed for 28 years.
d) He hasn't had more than four hours sleep a night since he became Prime Minister.
e) I haven't taken sleeping pills for ages.
f) A: How long have you been awake?
   B: Since three o'clock, dear.

## PRACTICE
### Present Perfect Continuous

**1**
a) He's been living in Spain since 1978.
b) He's been working for us for two weeks.
c) She's had the coat for 25 years.
d) They've known the Smiths since 1960.

**2**
Examples:
a) How long have you been living on the farm?
b) When did you last change the sheets?
c) Why did you decide not to come back downstairs?
d) What world events have you missed?
e) Have you had many visitors?
f) Why did you decide to wear rubber gloves?

## PRONUNCIATION
### Sentence stress

**1**
a) Telex.
b) Newspaper headline.
c) Telex.
d) Postcard.
e) Newspaper headline.

**2 and 3**
a) *I'm arriving at* Heathrow *on the* 10 p.m. flight. *Can you* meet *me*, please?
b) *There has been a* new spy scandal *and a* minister *has* resigned.
c) *Your* father *is* very ill. *You must* return immediately.
d) *We're* having *a* wonderful time. *The* weather *has been* amazing. *We've* visited Niagara Falls *and we're* visiting Hollywood *on* Tuesday.
e) *A* famous actor *has been* arrested *after his* wife *was* found dead.

**4 and 5**
a) street  b) cinema  c) coat  d) aspirin  e) personality

## SPEAKING

**1**
The 'popular' station is lighter and more familiar in tone, the language informal and colloquial. Music is sometimes used.
  The 'serious' station is more sober, solemn and serious. The content is of social importance and more factual.
  In both cases there was an introduction followed by interviews.

# Leisure

## Students' Book

**General theme:** leisure.
**Unit topic:** unusual hobbies.

**LISTENING:** people talking about their (unusual) hobbies.
**VOCABULARY:** words often confused (*take/bring*, etc.).

**LANGUAGE POINT 1:** obligation, prohibition and permission (*have to / don't have to, needn't, not allowed to, can/can't*).
**LANGUAGE POINT 2:** obligation and prohibition (*should, must, mustn't*).
**LANGUAGE POINT 3:** *must* or *have to* for personal and 'external' obligation.
**LANGUAGE POINT 4:** obligation, prohibition and permission in the past (*had to, could, was/were allowed to, didn't need to*).

**SPEAKING:** planning a leisure centre; discussing and presenting a poster.
**WRITING:** opening and closing a letter; re-ordering and writing a letter of request.

## Workbook

**READING:** re-ordering jumbled text describing a hobby.
**VOCABULARY:** synonyms; related groups of words; words often confused.
**GRAMMAR:** necessary or not necessary – *should, must, have to, mustn't, don't have to, needn't*; permission and prohibition – *(not) allowed to, can/can't, mustn't*; obligation, permission and prohibition in the past – *could, was/were allowed to, had to, didn't have to*.
**PRONUNCIATION:** weak forms (prepositions and auxiliary forms).
**WRITING:** punctuation and layout; abbreviations.

## Language

This unit is concerned with modal auxiliaries (see also Unit 9) and it might be worth reminding SS that modals express the speaker's (or listener's) opinion at the moment of speaking, and that they are followed by the base form of the verb. It is also necessary to make it clear that the same modal verb (e.g. *can*) can have a variety of different 'functions' (e.g. *ability, permission*, etc.). The 'functions' focused on in this unit are *obligation, permission* and *prohibition*.

By this level SS will probably have been exposed to most of the target language (*should, must, can, have to*, etc.). The problem will be understanding in which contexts to use one form and not the other.

## Common problems
### Obligation and absence of obligation
*Must/mustn't*

**1** Many SS overuse *must/mustn't* (*\*You must park your car over there.; \*You mustn't smoke.*) in situations where the imperative (with the appropriate intonation!) or *should/shouldn't* would sound less dogmatic. They also tend to use it in situations when *have to* would be more appropriate, e.g. *\*I must wear a uniform at school.*

**2** A common mistake is to follow *must/mustn't* by *to* (*\*I must to go.*), and also to use it for questions (*\*Must I do this?*) where *have to* (e.g. *Do I have to?*) would be more common. SS also have problems remembering to use *had to* (not *must*) for past obligation. They should also remember that they should use either *must* or *will have to* when referring to the future as *must* does not change its form.

**3** *Mustn't* is often used (mistakenly) to express an absence of obligation, instead of *needn't / don't have to* (*\*You mustn't wear a tie.*). This is often a Northern European problem.

**4** The pronunciation and weak forms of *must/mustn't* need highlighting (see the *Language reference*). The strong form of *must* is used for strong recommendations.

*Have (got) to / don't have to*

**1**   SS sometimes use *must* or *it is necessary* where *have to* is more appropriate (see above). Speakers of Latin languages also have a habit of saying *I am obliged to*, which is the wrong register.

**2**   SS get confused between the auxiliary form of *have* (*I've done my work.*) and *have to*. Unlike the auxiliary *have*, *have to* is used with *do* to make questions and negatives (*Do you have to? / I don't have to.*).

**3**   Although *have to* and *have got to* are more or less interchangeable, beware of SS saying *\*Do you have got to?* and (possible, but not very common) *\*I had got to.*

## LISTENING

### Before listening

● **Exercise 1**   Encourage SS to scan the adverts quickly to find the information required. The activity is intended as a warm-up for the *Listening* as well as an introduction to some of the vocabulary. Possibly discuss where the places in the adverts are, or show them on a map (Somerset, Northumberland, etc.) and make sure SS tell you the part of Britain you can go to for these holidays (e.g. Somerset) rather than the actual place of study (e.g. the name of the college).

● **Exercises 2 and 3**   An opportunity for personal response and opinion, which might include discussion on what, for example, a 'murder weekend' or a 'bee-keeping course' could involve. This activity could also be followed by a brainstorm of other hobbies.

### Listening

● **Exercise 1**   Ask SS what the attractions of these hobbies might be and try to elicit related vocabulary such as *honey, hive, insects,* etc.

● **Exercise 2**   This exercise simply asks the SS to identify the hobbies. Tell SS not to worry if they don't understand every word. SS have to listen quite hard to the recordings however. The speakers don't spell out what their hobbies are, but there are plenty of vocabulary clues – it might be worth asking SS to jot down any words they hear and then 'share their information' in groups to guess the hobby.

● **Exercise 3**   More intensive listening required. Some of the key language points of this unit (e.g. *don't have to*) come up in the listening text so possibly go directly to LANGUAGE POINT 1. If the recordings are too difficult for your group (the second and third might be a bit challenging because of the vocabulary load and the fact that the speakers have regional accents) let SS look at the tapescript (full edition of the SB only) and listen at the same time.

● **Exercise 4**   An opportunity to contrast ... *do you enjoy doing?* with ... *would you enjoy doing?*

## VOCABULARY

### Words which are often confused

● **Exercise 1**   SS could check their answers in a good dictionary, and look at the examples of how the particular words are used, not just the definitions.

● **Exercise 2**   Tell them to make a note of the words they got wrong in their vocabulary books. There are more of these in the WB, and also in SB Unit 17.

## LANGUAGE POINT 1

### Obligation and permission (1)

● **Exercise 1**   Focuses SS' attention on the use of the modal auxiliaries, and *allowed to*. Make sure SS understand words like 'obligation', 'permission' and 'prohibition'. SS need to be aware of the fact that some of the words and expressions practised are followed by the base form of the verb with *to* and some without *to* (e.g. *needn't **do***, but *have**to** **do***). Make sure that SS are using contracted forms, and refer them to the *Language reference* for the pronunciation of *must* and *have to*. Note also the elision of the *t* of *don't* in *don't have to* /dəunhæftə/.

# PRACTICE

● **Exercise 1**   As well as giving a lot of practice of the target language this exercise should generate a lot of vocabulary (e.g. vocabulary of driving, hospitals, marriage). Be prepared to help out here and/or encourage use of dictionaries. PW, and then exchange views in groups. SS could then report back to the rest of the class without naming the situation and another S can guess the situation. Example:

Student A: *'You have to get a visa and have injections. You don't have to take a lot of warm clothes with you.'*

Student B: *'Are you talking about visiting a tropical country?'*

# LANGUAGE POINT 2

## Obligation (2)

Make absolutely sure that SS realise how strong *you must* is, and that, in these examples, it is used only for emphasis or strong advice. Emphasise the fact that it is often used with *I* to remind yourself to do something. Give some practice in the stressed form of *must* and make sure that SS' intonation isn't too 'bossy'. Possibly introduce/revise *ought to* at the same time as *should*.

● **Exercise 1**   PW? In the feedback, stress the fact that *must/mustn't* are often seen in signs and formal notices. Get them to think of some situations, or provide some 'realia' yourself. If SS are in Britain you could get them to make a note of all the signs/notices with *must/mustn't.*

# LANGUAGE POINT 3

## *Must* or *have to*?

It might be better to do LANGUAGE POINTS 3 and 4 in a different lesson to LANGUAGE POINTS 1 and 2 as there is quite a heavy grammatical load in this unit which most SS will probably find excessive.

Since most SS tend to overuse *must* it is probably worthwhile encouraging them to use *have to* as much as possible, and trying to restrict *must* to *I* forms rather than spending too long on contrasting their uses. Possibly mention the use of *have got to*

here (see the *Language reference*). Make sure SS know how to ask questions and make the negative form of both *must* and *have to.*

# PRACTICE

● **Exercise 1**   Get SS to discuss their answers and why they chose them. Encourage SS to stress *must* in the examples.

# LANGUAGE POINT 4

## Obligation and permission (3)

● **Exercise 1**   A cued dictation which introduces the past forms of expressions practised earlier. You may like to pick up on what Jenny says about university life and compare what it is like in the SS' country/countries.

# PRACTICE

SS could also be asked to invent their own questionnaire using expressions of obligation, etc., either about the past or the present. This would work particularly well in a multinational class to find out information about other SS' countries, and in Britain SS could be asked to interview native speakers. The results of the interviews could then be written up in the form of a survey report.

# SPEAKING

As well as developing fluency this activity aims to get SS to use some of the vocabulary introduced in this unit, as well as expressions of obligation, prohibition, etc.

Use the photographs to elicit what a leisure centre is and what you'd expect to find there. Use SS' own experience. Elicit or introduce as much vocabulary as you can, including types of sports, entertainment, etc. Get agreement about what this leisure centre is aiming to do.

● **Exercise 1**  Look at the list of headings with SS before they begin their GW. Make sure they understand what the headings mean and start the ball rolling by eliciting/giving one or two examples of, e.g. possible forms of entertainment, types of restaurants and bars. Tell them to think of at least four different examples under each heading and remind them to make a note of the rules, opening hours, etc.

In their groups SS could design a poster to present to the rest of the class. One of the group could then use the poster as part of a 'presentation' to the rest of the class of what the leisure centre will have to offer. Vote on the best one.

# WRITING

## Opening and closing a letter

This activity revises work done on informal and semi-formal letters in Units 6 and 7 and focuses on functional/informal versus formal language in the context of the opening and closing of letters.

Possibly ask SS to write another letter based on the situations in the box (i.e. a job application, a letter of thanks, etc.) for extra practice. An opportunity here to do work on less 'grammatically generative' functional language, such as how to congratulate, complain, etc. In Britain SS could find some real adverts in a tourist brochure and write for information.

# Tapescripts

## RECORDING 1

MIKE: It's a very expensive hobby. It's going to cost about three and a half thousand, but you don't have to pay all at once. You know, you can pay each lesson as, as you go along. There's quite a lot of studying to do. In fact you're not allowed to go solo until you've got your air law exam and … But I enjoy the studying – that's one of the things that's, you know, been very, very exciting. And you have to do a lot of exams. Of course, you can't fly unless you're, you're fairly fit and you have to have a, a medical exam. In fact you can't go solo either until you've got your medical certificate.

JULIE: They're fascinating creatures and it's one of the hobbies that, once you get involved in you want to know more about, and however long you study bees and bee-, bee-keeping you'll never know everything about the insects. They have a, quite a unique lifestyle.

And of course there's always the benefits of taking the honey off at the end of the honey season, which makes a little profit, although it's quite an expensive hobby. You need quite a lot of equipment. The hives themselves are quite expensive, unless you're a good woodworker and can make them yourselves, and the extractors and things. But it keeps you occupied throughout the whole year because, while you're harvesting the honey in the summer, you're making up the hives and the frames in the winter, ready for the following season.

BRUCE: Well it's, it's something that anybody can participate in, from the keenest person like myself, who travels all over the world to see the birds, unto somebody looking out of the window in their kitchen, and there's so much involved in it. It gets you to places where you wouldn't normally go – i.e. some wild places, very remote places, because birds are attracted to the quieter, remoter places, usually – for example, up in, up into mountains and on river estuaries where not many people go, and also you meet such smashing people. Generally, well almost entirely, I think people interested in birds are nice sort of people.

## RECORDING 2

One of the things I liked most about going to university was living away from home, and the, and the freedom it gave me. So I could stay out as late as I wanted – I didn't have to explain to anyone where I'd been, and although we obviously had to do some work in order to get through the exams, well we didn't need to go to all the lectures if we didn't want to. Oh, it was incredibly relaxed; we were allowed to do whatever we wanted, within reason.

# Key

## LISTENING

### Before listening

**1**
a) London (Cheltenham).
b) The Lake District.
c) Cornwall.
d) Norfolk.
e) The Dales and Lake District.

### Listening

**1**
1 *Bee-keeping*: The Bee Inn, Northumberland.
2 *Birdwatching*: Dorset Coast Centre, Dorset.
3 *Flying*: Mortimer's Cross Inn in Bath.

**2**
Mike: Flying (3)
Julie: Bee-keeping (1)
Bruce: Birdwatching (2)

**3**

Mike
*Hobby*: Flying.
*Advantages*: The studying is exciting.
*Disadvantages*: It's expensive; there is a lot of studying.

Julie
*Hobby*: Bee-keeping.
*Advantages*: There is so much to learn; you can make a profit from the honey; it keeps you occupied all year.
*Disadvantages*: It's expensive.

Bruce
*Hobby*: Birdwatching.
*Advantages*: Everyone can participate; it gets you to different places; you meet lots of nice people.

## VOCABULARY

### Words which are often confused

**1**
a) bring   b) sensitive   c) lend   d) check   e) now
f) waiting for   g) watching   h) hear   i) lose

**2**
Examples:
a) Take the dog outside. He's making too much noise in here.
b) Sue would never do such a stupid thing: she's much too sensible.
c) I'm returning the £5 I borrowed from you yesterday.
d) I wish he would control his children better. They are always so naughty when visitors come.
e) I'm sorry I don't know. Actually, I'm a stranger here myself.
f) We are expecting the match to start at 3 o'clock.
g) Have you seen my keys anywhere?
h) Now listen to the instructions carefully. I'm not going to repeat them.
i) The handle is loose. Give me a screwdriver and I'll tighten it up.

## LANGUAGE POINT 1

### Obligation and permission (1)

Obligation: *have to*
No obligation: *don't have to, needn't*
Prohibition: *can't, not allowed to*
Permission: *can*

## PRACTICE

**2**
a) She has to feed the cat twice a day, put the rubbish out on a Thursday, send all the mail on to 68 Lanark Street, and pay the milkman on a Friday.
b) She isn't allowed to / can't park outside her neighbour's house, smoke, or stick things on the bedroom wall.

## LANGUAGE POINT 2

### Obligation (2)

**1**
a) 6   b) 5   c) 4   d) 7   e) 1   f) 3   g) 2

**2**
b) You aren't allowed in here dressed like that.
c) You mustn't talk in the library.
d) You can't play unless you're a member.
e) You mustn't feed the animals.

**3**
a) I must get to the shops before they close.
b) You can't / aren't allowed to have dogs in flats.
c) You aren't allowed to play loud music after 11 p.m.
d) You have to wear school uniform.
e) You mustn't work so hard.

## PRACTICE

### *Must* or *have to?*

**1**
a) have to   b) must   c) must   d) have to
e) have to   f) must

**2**
b) mustn't   c) mustn't   d) don't have to

## LANGUAGE POINT 4

### Obligation and permission (3)

**1**
1 could   2 didn't have to   3 had to
4 didn't need to   5 were allowed

**2**
a) had to   b) had to   c) didn't need to
d) could   e) were allowed to

## WRITING

### Opening and closing a letter

**1**
b) personal – sympathy
c) personal – thanks
d) semi-formal – asking for information
e) semi-formal – ordering goods
f) personal – congratulations
g) formal – job application

**2**
Semi-formal: a), b), d), f)
Personal: c), e)

**3**
a) 5,   b) 4,   c) 1,   d) 2

**4**
Likely order of paragraphs: 4, 1, 5, 2, 3

# A meal or murder?

## Students' Book

**General theme:** animals.
**Unit topic:** food and health.

**READING:** magazine article: a meat-eater and a vegetarian explain their attitudes to eating meat.
**VOCABULARY:** deducing words in context; the grammar of phrasal verbs.

**LANGUAGE POINT:** quantity expressions (e.g. *some, any*); (giving advice).
**PRONUNCIATION:** consonants (voiced versus unvoiced).

**SPEAKING:** survey of eating habits.
**WRITING:** writing a report of the survey.

## Workbook

**VOCABULARY 1:** food expressions (e.g. *a box of, a loaf of*).
**LISTENING:** someone talking about his eating habits.
**GRAMMAR:** countable versus uncountable nouns; quantity expressions.
**VOCABULARY 2:** eating and drinking; phrasal verbs.
**WRITING:** writing a campaign advertisement against animal cruelty.

## Language

The main focus of this unit is on quantity. At this level it is easy to think SS 'know' quantity expressions because they recognise them. However, they are rarely used accurately. The first problem for SS is that the distinction between countable and uncountable (mass) nouns in English is not always obvious. SS will often need to check in the dictionary. (A good dictionary will indicate *C* or *U*.)

## Common problems
### Countable or uncountable?

**1**  Some words can be both countable and uncountable (e.g. *a piece of chicken / two chickens*).

**2**  A considerable number of words are uncountable in English (e.g. *news* and *furniture*) but countable in many other languages.

**3**  In most other languages the distinction between e.g. *some/any* (see the *Language reference*) doesn't exist (**There are any eggs in the fridge.*). The other distinctions (*much/many, few / a few*, etc.) also need a lot of practice.

**4**  Confusion between *no* (determiner: *There's no sugar left.*) and *none* (pronoun: *There's none left.*).

**5**  In Japanese and Chinese, for example, there is no clear singular/plural distinction and therefore no countable/uncountable distinction either.

### Phrasal verbs
Some phrasal verbs (see Unit 10) are transitive (i.e. followed by a direct object), and the verb and the particle can be separated, except:
– when the object is a pronoun: *They put off their visit. / They put their visit off. / They put it off.* (but not **They put off it.*).
– when the particle is a preposition: *I got round my parents.* (not **I got my parents round.*).

Intransitive phrasal verbs (i.e. those not followed by a direct object) cannot be separated by another adverb (e.g. *They got up early.* not **They got early up.*).

  SS need a lot of exposure and practice if they are

to use phrasal verbs naturally. However, it's much better to do a small amount of work on them regularly than long one-off sessions. The same goes for the grammatical rules outlined above: small doses are preferable. As for the meaning/use of specific phrasal verbs, work on them in context: it makes them more memorable and helps SS use them appropriately.

## Consonants

**1** In some languages (e.g. German), voiced sounds like /ʒ/ and /dʒ/ do not occur at the ends of words. In fact, the whole voiced/unvoiced distinction is a problem and can interfere with communication (e.g. as when words like *pear/ bear, rice/rise, leaf/leave, pup/pub* are confused).

**2** There is no exact equivalence of all consonant phonemes with those in SS' own language (e.g. the /θ/ and /ð/ sounds do not occur in Turkish).

**3** Some SS find it difficult to distinguish between particular consonants (/l/ and /r/ for the Japanese).

**4** Consonant clusters (when two or more consonants occur together (e.g. **str**eet, doe**sn't**) are very difficult for many SS.

# READING

## Before reading

Encourage prediction of Kerry and Helen's arguments. Possibly open up mini-discussion on vegetarianism (the pros/cons and the reasons) and ask SS how much it is practised in their country.

## Reading

● **Exercise 1** If there are no (or very few) vegetarians in your class, you might have to get some meat-eaters to read Text B. Alternatively, divide the class and have one half read one article, the other half the other, so that it remains a 'jigsaw activity'. If necessary, treat the texts as separate reading tasks.

Since the VOCABULARY section which follows practises deduction of words in context, discourage use of dictionaries at this stage. However, before SS read, possibly elicit differences between: *cow/beef, thin/skinny*. Possibly ask SS to underline any new words they come across.

You might like to have a follow-up discussion on pros/cons of vegetarianism.

# VOCABULARY

## Deducing words in context

● **Exercise 1** This demands that SS look at the general sense of the words in context. For one or two items (e.g. Text A, item b) ask SS for reasons for their deductions. If they can't deduce, they should look in their dictionaries.

● **Exercise 2** Check answers in a dictionary and practise pronunciation.

● **Exercise 3** A follow-up to Unit 10. Apart from the PRACTICE section which follows there is a further exercise in the WB. SS need to practise using a (monolingual) dictionary to explore the use of phrasal verbs (and their many meanings). Possibly, play down SS having to *understand* the 'rules' of the transitive/intransitive distinction (see *Language* above, though it is not actually practised in the unit) and the adverb/preposition distinction. Concentrate instead on dictionary examples and practice (and SS making a record in their vocabulary books). The dictionary can often help with whether a verb is transitive (*T*) or intransitive (*I*) and where the adverb/preposition can go if the verb is transitive. Point out to SS the assimilation of *t* with *r* in *get round* and the linking of the consonant to the vowel in *put off.* Perhaps practise the 'linking' of consonant to vowel in the phrasal verbs in the PRACTICE activity.

# LANGUAGE POINT

## Quantity

Possibly do some revision first on:
- units of measurement: e.g. *pound/kilo, pint/litre, dozen.*
- expressions like *a loaf of ..., a tin of ...* (see WB).
- distinction between countable/uncountable nouns (see WB).

● **Exercises 1 and 2** These require SS to make deductions from examples before formulating the 'rules' in Exercise 4.

# PRACTICE

● **Exercise 1** To make it extra difficult try it in alphabetical order: *an apple, some biscuits, three cakes* ... It's fun but tough.

● **Exercise 2** A lot of the vocabulary needed for Exercise 4 should come up here. Make sure SS understand the names of the meals.

● **Exercise 3** Practises quantity expressions.

● **Exercise 4** Before doing this exercise, let SS use their dictionaries for unknown words or work in pairs and help each other understand. Notice that this links in with LANGUAGE POINT 3 in Unit 8 (*very / too / not enough*).

● **Exercise 5** In Unit 9 if you introduced expressions for giving advice (e.g. *I think you'd better* ...), you could revise them here.

● **Exercise 6** Fun if more 'free practice' is needed; otherwise *optional.*

# PRONUNCIATION

## Consonants

The voiced/unvoiced distinction has been made in the PRONUNCIATION section of Review Units 2 and 3 (Present and Past Simple endings). Point out that all vowels are 'voiced'?

● **Exercise 3** Obviously inauthentic dialogues, which are intended to focus on sounds not vocabulary! Get SS to exaggerate and have fun practising them.

# SPEAKING

● **Exercise 1** Explain: *additives, vitamin supplements, 'live to eat'* (versus *'eat to live'*).

Possibly look at pros/cons of each issue (e.g. the pros and cons of diets, additives, salt, etc.).

The questionnaire could be extended to include a *Why?* column. In Britain the survey could be conducted on native speakers.

# WRITING

## Writing a report

● **Exercise 1** Get SS to help each other with words like: *staggering, snacks, fizzy, irresistible.* Explain what a British *'fry-up'* is (i.e. eggs, sausages, bacon, fried bread, etc. – less common these days). Compare with SS' own breakfasts.

● **Exercise 3** Give SS an example.

# Tapescripts

## RECORDING 1

ANDREW: What sort of things do I buy? Well, I buy lots of meat because it makes me feel full of energy … and it's nice. I buy very little other fresh food, though. I prefer my meals out of the freezer. But I do like fruit, so on Thursdays I go to the market and get some apples, bananas, melons … things like that. I know I don't eat many vegetables. The trouble is there aren't any vegetables I really like. Anyway, I, I have hardly any time for cooking these days.

BRIGITTE: Well, I can't eat food with additives – none at all – so when I'm in a supermarket I have to spend a lot of time looking at labels. Actually, I, I don't eat much tinned food. Or, or even frozen food. I prefer everything fresh. And as for sweet things, they're not very good for you so I never have any chocolates or things like that in the house – although sometimes I, I do buy a few home-made biscuits from a friend. What else? Oh, I like dairy products, particularly milk and yoghurt. And, oh yes, every Saturday I buy a little cheese as a treat. I try not to eat too many eggs, though. I don't want a heart attack!

## RECORDING 2

zoo, six, jam, church, shoe, usual, this, both

## RECORDING 3

a) A: Pass the scissors, Susan.
   B: Say 'please', stupid. Or else!

b) A: Jim and Charles chose a large gin with a cherry.
   B: Charming! Put cheap ginger jam on their cheese.

c) A: I usually wear short, beige shirts.
   B: With your shape, you should wear something less casual and fashionable!

d) A: Thank your mother and father for their sympathy.
   B: I don't think it's worth bothering either of them.

# Key

## READING

### Before reading

**2**

*Vegetarian* (doesn't eat meat).
*Vegan* (doesn't eat any animal products).

### Reading

*Text A: Helen's point of view*
a) … she thought of meat as animals and it made her feel guilty.
b) … telling them she would be sick if she ate meat.
c) … free-range eggs and cheese.
d) … is healthy.

*(Kerry)*
1 Kerry feels that eating meat is healthier because you get enough protein and don't need to take vitamin tablets and don't get too skinny.
2 She doesn't eat rabbit unless it has already been chopped up.
3 She doesn't wear fur.
4 It's natural for humans to eat meat.

*Text B: Kerry's point of view*
a) … you get a lot of protein from meat.
b) … she sees rabbits as pets.
c) … wear leather.
d) … some animals are killed only for their fur and not for meat, which is natural.
e) … animals are not tortured when they are killed and she doesn't think of meat as an animal when she sees it on the plate.

*(Helen)*
1 Helen gave up eating meat a year and a half ago. It happened when she started thinking of it as eating an animal rather than a piece of meat.
2 Her mother didn't like the idea but her father agreed. Her mother took her to the doctor to get advice.
3 Chickens and turkeys are the worst to eat because it's easy to think of them as whole animals.
4 She eats (free-range) eggs and cheese at home and soya meals at school.
5 She feels very proud.

**2**
Examples from Helen: *that's OK by me* (paragraph 2); *I do get a bit of stick* (paragraph 3)
Examples from Kerry: The short sentence without a verb: *A bit hypocritical* (paragraph 3); *That's OK* (paragraph 3)

## VOCABULARY

### Deducing words in context

**1**
Text A
a) ii)  b) ii)  c) ii)  d) i)  e) i)

Text B
a) i)  b) i)  c) ii)  d) ii)  e) i

**3**
a)  Definition 3
b)  Definition 4

## PRACTICE

**1**
a)  smoking
b)  my coat
c)  the baby
d)  the music
e)  going to college next year

The particle can also come after the object in b) and d).
b)  I took my coat off.
d)  I turned the music up.

## LANGUAGE POINT

### Quantity

**1**
*Andrew*
… I buy <u>much</u> (*lots of*) meat because …
… I buy very <u>few</u> (*little*) other fresh food …
… get <u>any</u> (*some*) apples …
… I don't eat <u>much</u> (*many*) vegetables.
… there aren't <u>some</u> (*any*) vegetables …
… I have hardly <u>some</u> (*any*) time for cooking …

*Brigitte*
… additives – <u>no any</u> (*none*) at all …
… I don't eat <u>many</u> (*much*) tinned food.
… I never have <u>some</u> (*any*) chocolates …
… I do buy <u>a little</u> (*a few*) home-made biscuits …
… every Saturday I buy <u>a few</u> (*a little*) cheese …
I try not to eat too <u>much</u> (*many*) eggs …

**4**
a)  i)   We use **some** in affirmative sentences:
         *I want **some** bread.*
     ii)  We use **any** in sentences with a negative meaning:
         *I never drink **any** alcohol. I don't want **any** mineral water, thanks.*
     iii) In requests and offers when we want the answer:
         *Yes* we use **some**:
         *Would you like **some** cake?*

b)  i)   We use **much** and **a little** with uncountable nouns:
         *'Is there **much** wine left?'*
         *'No, there's only **a little**.'*
     ii)  We use **many** and **a few** with countable nouns:
         *There are not **many** cans of beer left and there are only **a few** cartons of orange juice.*

## PRONUNCIATION

### Consonants

**2**
Voiced consonants: /z/, /dʒ/, /ʒ/, /ð/
Unvoiced consonants:  /s/, /tʃ/, /ʃ/, /θ/

**3**
b)  /dʒ/ and /tʃ/
c)  /ʒ/ and /ʃ/
d)  /ð/ and /θ/

## WRITING

### Writing a report

**1**
(The linking expressions referred to in Exercise 3 are shown in italics.)

According to a recent Health Authority survey, eating habits among <u>the great majority</u> of teenagers are changing for the better. *However*, the habit of eating <u>too many</u> sweet foods still persists.

The report found that <u>a third of</u> 11-year-old boys and <u>two-thirds of</u> 11-year-old girls are on a diet. *However*, <u>two out of three</u> boys still eat fried food at least every other day, *although* a staggering <u>seventy-five per cent</u> now prefer to eat healthier cereal and wholemeal bread for breakfast rather than the traditional British 'fry-up'. *In addition*, <u>almost all</u> young people appear to be cutting down on food such as hamburgers and sausages. *Nevertheless*, <u>over half of</u> those interviewed still eat meat every day.

The report concluded that, despite <u>much more</u> awareness of healthier eating among the 11–16 age group, sweet snacks are still the weakness for <u>most</u> young people. <u>Four out of five</u> teenagers still find fizzy drinks, crisps and chocolate irresistible and <u>hardly any</u> of the teenagers said they would give them up.

**2**
Most teenagers are now eating more healthily, but most still also like sweet snacks.

# Beastly tales

## Students' Book

**General theme:** animals.
**Unit topic:** unusual pets.

**VOCABULARY 1:** animal vocabulary.
**LISTENING:** interview with a woman who keeps tarantulas.

**LANGUAGE POINT 1:** reported statements.
**LANGUAGE POINT 2:** reported questions.
**LANGUAGE POINT 3:** reported imperatives.

**VOCABULARY 2:** expressions with *like*; idiomatic 'animal' expressions describing people.
**SPEAKING:** expanding a story; adjectives connected to photographs and poems; writing a poem.

## Workbook

**READING:** quiz; factual information about tarantulas.
**GRAMMAR:** reported statements and questions; reporting verbs (e.g. *advise*, *invite*, etc.).
**VOCABULARY:** animal names; classifying words.
**WRITING:** changing a summary to direct speech.
**PRONUNCIATION:** problem consonants.

## Language

The focus in this unit is on reported speech. In most cases the problems for SS will be that of form rather than meaning and will involve work on tenses and word order.

## Common problems
### Reported statements

**1** *Say* and *tell* cause problems because one is followed by an object and the other isn't (\**I said him that*, \**I told to him.*). Further confusion arises because *tell* is also used to report imperatives, but with a different construction, e.g. *She told him that the taxi had arrived.* (statement); *She told him to hurry up.* (imperative). In almost all other languages there is one word for *say* and *tell*.

**2** SS frequently forget to 'backshift' with tenses (although when statements are still true this doesn't matter), and forget which modals change their form when reported (see the *Language reference*).

**3** Sometimes the exact words don't need to be reported, e.g. '*Let's go for a walk.*' becomes *She suggested we went (should go) for a walk.*

**4** Statements are often reported with verbs other than *tell* and *say* (e.g. *suggest, complain, apologise, offer*) and in this case the sentence structure may change (e.g. *She apologised for being late.*). To avoid confusion these other reporting verbs have not been included in the SB (see *Upper Intermediate Matters*), but there are some examples in the WB.

### Reported questions

**1** SS often still include *do/did* (\**He asked me where did I live.*), or keep the inversion with *be/have* (\**He asked me where was I living.*).

**2** *Ask* can be confusing because it takes an indirect object in most other languages (\**I asked to him.*). It reports both statements (*I asked him whether he …*) and imperatives, (*I asked her to be early.*). It needs several different verbs to translate all its major uses.

**3** Either *if* or *whether* can be used when reporting *Yes/No* questions.

### Reported imperatives

Imperatives are usually reported by using a reporting verb *tell, ask, persuade*, etc. and indirect object and infinitive / negative infinitive (*I told him (not) to get up.*). *Say* is not usually used.

# VOCABULARY 1

● **Exercise 1**  Possibly follow this vocabulary activity up with the 'animals vocabulary' exercise in the WB, or VOCABULARY 2. Alternatively, to tie in the work on consonants done in Unit 15, and revise the phonemic script, dictate or write on the board a list of words, such as the following, for SS to transcribe: *sat* (/sæt/), *sauce* (/sɔːs/), *dig* (/dɪg/), fear /fɪə/), *house* (/haʊs/).

SS should then change a consonant in order to make the name of an animal which has the same pronunciation (e.g. *cat, horse, pig, deer, mouse*).

● **Exercise 2**  Some vocabulary may need explaining here (e.g. *hamster, squirrel, gobbled up, shed*). Scope for revision of *have* versus *would like* here (e.g. concept questions on the texts, such as *'Has Lewis got a squirrel?' 'Has Rosemary got a tiger?'* – *'No, but they'd like (to have) one.'*) and revision of conditional clauses (e.g. *'If Rosemary had a tiger what would she call it?'*). This could also be extended into a discussion of pets SS themselves would like.

# LISTENING

## Before listening

● **Exercise 1, a)**  An opportunity to introduce the word *tarantula*. Draw SS' attention to Ann Webb's surname!

● **Exercise 1, c)**  Revision of question forms. Possibly see if SS remember how to ask less direct questions (revision from Review Unit 1).

## Listening

● **Exercises 1 and 2**  Exercise 1 is listening for gist. Exercise 2 requires SS to listen for specific information. If SS find the text too difficult to

understand let them read the tapescript (full edition of the SB only) at the same time. You may want to explain some of the more difficult vocabulary (e.g. *awe, cockroach, obnoxious, burrow*).

● **Exercise 3**  This requires intensive listening and leads into reported statements (LANGUAGE POINT 1). However, when SS report back don't worry too much about the accuracy of their reported statements at this stage. Concentrate instead on the use of contrastive stress (e.g. *'No, **90%** of the population would be terrified.'*).

# LANGUAGE POINT 1

## Reported statements

● **Exercise 1**  Make sure SS look at the rules for reported statements in the *Language reference*. They will probably need to refer to them during the PRACTICE.

● **Exercise 2**  Possibly mention to SS that other reporting verbs such as *offer, agree*, etc. are also used and that some are followed by an object and some aren't.

# PRACTICE

● **Exercise 2**  This activity could be extended by roleplaying the dialogue between the reporter and Susan Kirkwood, basing it on the newspaper report and trying to use the exact words. Explain or get SS to look up words like *eccentric, ironic, pension*. An alternative approach is to let SS try to complete the text before they listen, by guessing what was said in the interview, and then listening to check their answers.

Possibly go on to the VOCABULARY and/or the SPEAKING section(s) if you have time, rather than attempting reported questions at this stage. Some SS might find too much focus on grammatical form rather 'heavy'.

## LANGUAGE POINT 2

### Reported questions

Try to get SS to work out the rules for reported questions by attempting Exercise 2. Then check with the *Language reference*.

## PRACTICE

This activity gives practice in direct questions as well as reported ones. Perhaps give an example first. Possible topics could be what SS did last night, where they're going on holiday, what they had for lunch, etc.

## LANGUAGE POINT 3

### Reported imperatives

If you feel that SS might have forgotten the original LISTENING, you may prefer to think of your own examples to illustrate reported imperatives (based on the classroom situation?).

● **Exercise 2**  Possibly write up on the board the example of a reported imperative, (e.g. *Ann persuaded me to stroke Cleo.*) and elicit the grammatical rule to write below the example (e.g. subject + reporting verb + object + *to* + base form) for easy reference. Or refer them to the *Language reference*. If you want to do further practice of this construction there is an exercise in the WB.

## PRACTICE

PW: SS compare their answers in pairs. A good opportunity, if necessary, to do revision of reported statements and questions. There is an additional exercise in the WB.

## VOCABULARY 2

● **Exercise 1**  Impress upon SS that it is usually better for a non-native speaker not to use these expressions – they can sound odd, and some of them are getting dated. However it can be an amusing exercise in the classroom and good for recognition purposes. Possibly compare this exercise with the *as … as* exercise in Unit 8 and perhaps introduce a few 'animal' expressions with *as … as* (e.g. *as weak as a kitten, as cunning as a fox, as blind as a bat*, etc.).

● **Exercise 2**  Perhaps elicit characteristics of the various animals concerned before trying to do the matching exercise.

## SPEAKING

● **Exercises 1–4**  These activities focus on oral fluency – don't worry too much if SS make mistakes. Can be done as PW/GW. SS need to use their imagination – some classes will need you to start them off, and they may need some help with the vocabulary. Possibly tell SS one of the original versions of the story *How the leopard got its spots* at the end.

(The leopard, along with a lot of other animals, was accompanying the ant to his mother's funeral. On the way, they passed a farm, where there were lots of fresh eggs, which the leopard loved. When the other animals weren't looking he rushed into the farm and ate half of the eggs. The farmer saw the animals and blamed them, but they denied it and agreed to stand trial. The farmer made a big fire, and told the animals to jump over it, saying that the guilty one would fall into the fire. Of course the leopard fell in, and that's why he has a spotted coat – as a reminder of his greed.)

## CREATIVE WRITING

• **Exercise 1** SS could be asked to check the meaning of the words in the box in their dictionaries and mark the stress and check the pronunciation. PW/GW: SS compare their adjectives and justify why they chose them. Again, the focus is on oral fluency.

• **Exercise 2** Possibly read these poems out aloud to SS, so that they can feel the dramatic impact. Ask them which one they prefer, and whether the writer is positive or negative towards the animals.

• **Exercise 3** Write the headings (*appearance, behaviour, personality* and *movement*) on the board, and get SS to note down as many words as they can connected to 'their' animal, before they try to write something. PW/GW?

Another possible activity is to divide SS into groups and get each group of SS to write down as many sentences as they can connected to a particular animal. Then they should choose the best sentences from the 'pool' to make a poem from. Each group could then read out their poem and have a vote on which is the best.

As an extension activity, take in other animal poems. Another suggestion is to get SS to write the name of an animal or bird down the side of a piece of paper and write a line beginning with the letter. Example:

*Every evening*
*A ...*
*G ...*
*L ...*
*E ...*

# Tapescripts

### RECORDING 1

ANNOUNCER: It's 11.47 and now *Pet Subjects*. Fergus Keeling explores the special relationship between people and their pets. For the first programme in the series he visits Ann Webb at her home in Hertfordshire.

INTERVIEWER: I've come to see Ann's collection of spiders. Tarantulas mostly, Ann, are they?

ANN WEBB: They're all tarantulas, yes. They're all the big hairy spiders.

I: How many do you have?

A: There's about 80 at the moment.

I: When did you buy the first one?

A: About 1982 we bought the first one.

I: And I know your, your husband Frank is also quite passionate about spiders.

A: Oh, absolutely, yeah. He's passionate about all animals, not just spiders.

I: Are, are these animals pets?

A: They are to me, yes. They're, they're all part of my family. So therefore they're pets. They're not to everyone, of course. I mean, some, some people study spiders for scientific research and various other reasons, I suppose, and a lot of people don't have, accept them as pets, but I do, and most of mine have got names.

I: What do they feed on, Ann?

A: Well they feed on live insects which is perhaps a thing that would put off a lot of people from keeping them, but mine feed mostly on house crickets because they're easy enough to breed. But they'll eat locusts and they'll eat cockroaches and anything obnoxious really.

I: So when, when is feeding time?

A: We feed ours once a week, because that's all they need. I mean, in the wild they'll sometimes go six months, a year, without feeding, because they don't stray from their burrows – they sit there and wait for the food to come to them. Of course it doesn't always come.

### RECORDING 2

I: Is it possible for you to take one out?

AW: Yeah, we'll get Cleo out for you.

I: What do you actually get from a moment like this when you're sitting holding Cleo?

A: Probably sounds silly, but I'm almost in awe of my spiders. To me they are so beautiful and so graceful. I actually get lost for words when I'm holding a spider.

I: You're sitting here quite calmly and, and this tarantula's covering both your hands. Now some people listening will be shuddering at the very idea, of course.

A: Of course they will. Of course they will. Most people will. I should think 90 per cent of the population would be absolutely terrified.

I: Is that terror justified?

A: No, these spiders have got a very, very bad press. James Bond films, *Raiders of the Lost Ark*, etc. made it worse, and newspapers do their best to make it even worse still because they believe that these spiders are deadly and they're not. There is not a tarantula in the world that will kill a human being. Their bite – if they do bite, which they don't, they don't – they're not naturally aggressive towards anything so they don't bite just because they want, they feel like it, but if they do, then it's the equivalent of a bee sting, and that is all. This is another Mexican red-knee. This is Arabella, and she's quite a sweetie. Hello darling, aren't you – you're very sweet.

I: You're obviously completely passionate about spiders, aren't you, Ann. (Oh, yeah.) Why?

A: Don't know. That's an awful answer, isn't it, but it's true. I'm often asked that – 'Why do you like them?' I don't really know, I just do. I like their beauty and their grace and their individuality – their peaceful lifestyle. I just love them.

## RECORDING 3

REPORTER: Mrs Kirkwood, what did your aunt leave to you in her will?

MRS KIRKWOOD: Er, £350 and a photo album! But then even her cats haven't got anything. She obviously wanted to leave it all to dear old Fred, who got £26,000.

R: What was your reaction when you heard the news?

MRS K: Well, the thing is you've got to understand that Dolly was very eccentric and so the family aren't a bit surprised. Mind you, it's ironic that we will have to go on living off my £100 a week pension, while Fred will be able to have a life of luxury.

R: And what do you think Fred will do with the money?

MRS K: Unfortunately, the only things he can spend it on are his favourite lettuce, tomatoes and courgettes! But we're not bitter – I'll look after Fred as well as I can – although probably not quite as well as she did!

# Key

## VOCABULARY 1

**1**
1 ferret
2 tiger
3 rat
4 bat
5 crocodile
6 snake

**2**
a) Pets they have: *hamster, worms.*
Pets they would like to have: *kitten, squirrel, alligator, tiger.*

## LISTENING

### Before listening

a) Tarantula.

### Listening

**2**
a) 80
b) 1982
c) loves all animals, including spiders
d) treats them as part of the family
e) eat lots of different insects
f) breeds them herself
g) every week
h) wait for food to arrive

**3**
(Mistakes underlined; corrections in *italics*.)

Mrs Webb told me that while she was holding a spider she often felt too afraid to speak (*she felt too in awe of the spider to speak*). She said that 60 per cent (*90 per cent*) of the population would also be terrified. However, she said that films such as James Bond films had given spiders good publicity (*bad publicity*). She said that tarantulas could sting a human being like a bee (*they occasionally bite but it's only the equivalent of a bee sting*) if they felt like it and, although they were not naturally aggressive, they would kill a person if necessary (*no tarantula would kill a human being*). Ann said she liked their beauty and their exciting lifestyle (*their grace and individuality*) but she didn't know why she was so passionate about them.

## LANGUAGE POINT 1

### Reported statements

**2**
*Tell* must always be followed by an object: *I told him that ...* (NOT *I told that ...*).

## PRACTICE

**2**
a) had left
b) 350
c) hadn't
d) had wanted
e) had been / was
f) weren't / hadn't been
g) would
h) would
i) could
j) were
k) did / had done

## LANGUAGE POINT 2

### Reported questions

**1**
'When did you buy the first one?'
'Do you like spiders?'

**2**
a) … do not take the auxiliary *do/does/did*.
b) … is a statement.
c) … changes.
d) … usually changes into the past.

**3**
When reporting *Yes/No* questions use *if* or *whether*.

## LANGUAGE POINT 3

### Reported imperatives

**1**
a) ii) tell
   iii) invite
   iv) ask
b) ii) Ann told him not to drop her or she would hurt herself.
   iii) Ann invited him to pick her up if he wanted to.
   iv) Ann asked him to give Cleo that insect to eat.

**2**
AFFIRMATIVE
subject + reporting verb + object + *to* + base form

**3**
NEGATIVE
subject + reporting verb + object + *not* + *to* + base form

## PRACTICE

a) He asked her why the shop had closed already.
b) The fortune-teller told me that I would meet …
c) The doctor told him to avoid …
d) Susan said she had just seen …
e) The teacher asked Peter to open …
f) They tried to persuade me not to go.
g) Richard invited Christine to stay for dinner.
h) Jennifer said (that) the tennis match hadn't finished yet.

## VOCABULARY 2

**1**
a)
'To have eyes like a hawk' means 'to have very sharp eyes'.
'To work like a dog' means 'to work very hard'.
'To drink like a fish' means 'to be a big drinker – usually of alcohol'.
'To eat like a horse' means 'to have a very big appetite'.

**2**
a)
batty: mad/crazy
sheepish: self-conscious/embarrassed
ratty/crabby: irritable
cat's whiskers: arrogant/conceited
mousy: shy/quiet
bee's knees: arrogant/conceited

# What are you afraid of ?

## Language

The suffix -ing is very important in English and causes many problems. This unit deals mainly with the contrast between verbs which are followed by -ing (see also Review Unit 1: *I enjoy reading*.) and verbs followed by *to* + base form (*I decided to go*.). Because of mother tongue 'interference', -ing and *to* + base form are frequently mixed up.

In this unit, there is also some awareness work and practice of the -ing form in adjectives and nouns. (When -ing participles are used as nouns they are sometimes called 'gerunds'.) In some languages (e.g. French) the infinitive (or an abstract noun giving the same meaning) is used rather than an -ing form. Note that -ing nouns operate in the same way as other nouns (e.g. they can take the article, a pronoun and be made plural: *the/my feelings*). However, at this level, it is probably not worth spending too much time on this aspect.

Notice that the unit also practises verbs which can be followed by either -ing or *to* + base form with little change of meaning. It does *not* practise those verbs where there *is* a change of meaning (e.g. *remember, forget, try*, etc.) (see *Upper Intermediate Matters*).

### Diphthongs

In Unit 10 vowels (i.e. monophthongs) were practised. Here the pronunciation focus is on diphthongs. SS will need to recognise that whereas in monophthongs the tongue/lips hold their position; in diphthongs the lip/tongue position gradually changes (i.e. the tongue glides from one position to another within a single syllable).

### Common problems

**1** There are fewer diphthongs in some languages than in English (e.g. French) and in other languages (e.g. Swahili) fewer vowels. Many SS find it difficult to distinguish between English diphthongs (e.g. *bow* /əʊ/ and *bough* /aʊ/) and between monophthongs and diphthongs (e.g. *law* /ɔː/ and *low* /əʊ/). Many SS (e.g. Thais) often pronounce some diphthongs as pure vowels (/e/ instead of /eɪ/).

**2**  Some SS (e.g. Italians) tend to give equal weight to the two elements of the diphthong (in English, greater weight is given to the first element).

# READING

## Before reading

Examples of common phobias: enclosed spaces (claustrophobia), open spaces (agorophobia), heights (acrophobia), water (hydrophobia), spiders (arachnophobia), thunder (brontophobia).

   Probably better *not* to ask SS their phobias at this stage. Wait until they are more relaxed with the topic and then possibly build it up into a more extended speaking activity (e.g. a questionnaire which also refers to symptoms/cure, etc. after LANGUAGE POINT 1).

## Reading

● **Exercise 1**  Get SS to work without dictionaries.

● **Exercise 2**  Encourage SS to deduce/guess words from context (e.g. *irrational, phobics, pounding, nausea, thumps, spotted*) and then check in their dictionaries. Possibly, take in (a picture of) some rhubarb. Discuss what a *rational fear* might be. Some work on illness symptoms was done in Unit 9. There is a related listening exercise in the WB (interview with four people about their fears).

# VOCABULARY

## Adjectives into verbs

● **Exercise 1**  Notice the words connected to fear are adjectives and end in *-ed*. Possibly get SS to try the exercise (PW?) before checking their answers in the dictionary. There is more work on the 'vocabulary of fear' in the WB. There is also more work on changing adjectives into verbs.

# PRONUNCIATION

## Diphthongs

Notice not all English diphthongs are focused on in this unit. Two of the diphthongs (*sou*nds, *go*) finish on the /ʊ/ sound (lips moving to a rounded, as though whistling position), the other two (*way*, *fly*) finish on the /ɪ/ sound (the lips more spread, as though smiling).

● **Exercises 1–5**  These exercises could all be done as PW/GW. Note that the focus is on recognition, but make sure SS also *practise* the diphthongs. If it is helpful, draw their attention to the difference between the 'start' position and the 'finish' position (showing the shape of the jaw as it closes can sometimes be useful). Possibly also practise saying the sentences in Exercise 4. You could extend this exercise by giving SS other words which they have to put into the correct columns. Alternatively, model other diphthongs, getting SS to put words containing those diphthongs into columns (one sound for each column). Then have SS check their answers in the dictionary and practise their pronunciation of the words.

# LANGUAGE POINT 1

## The *-ing* form

Notice that the exercises mix the use of *-ing* as a noun (*the shopping*),  an adjective (*moving*), a participle in the Past Continuous (*was driving*) and *-ing* clauses (*gripping the side of my bag*).

# PRACTICE

● **Exercise 1**  Possibly link to a phobia questionnaire as suggested in the notes for *Before reading* above.

● **Exercise 2**  Either PW/GW or check answers in pairs.

## LANGUAGE POINT 2

### -ing or to?

Notice that the answers to all the SB and WB exercises on this issue can be found in the *Language reference*. Don't draw SS' attention to this until they have tried the exercises.

In the *Language reference* the point about many verbs followed by *to* + base form referring to the future could be balanced by the statement that many verbs followed by *-ing* often refer to the present or the immediate past. However, there are many exceptions, so it is better to present SS with lots of examples rather than 'rules'. A lot of on-going practice is also needed and the WB exercise is recommended.

Get SS to have a section in their vocabulary books for the two types of verb and encourage them to add to it whenever they can.

## PRACTICE

● **Exercise 1**   Aims to give oral practice in making choices in a semi-restricted way. Possibly do some examples with the whole class to get the activity going and to give ideas for different types of responses. Accuracy is all-important, so go over what SS have done at the end and get them to divide the verbs into the two categories.

## SPEAKING

### Before speaking

● **Exercise 1**   Explain that one text talks about someone's phobia; the other talks about Professor Marks' suggested techniques for a cure. Refer SS back to the previous text for information about Professor Marks. Ask if SS know anyone with a button phobia. (A serious problem for many people.)

Give Students A and B enough time to read and understand 'their' texts. Encourage use of dictionary since some words might be a problem (e.g. *fastenings, cardigans, cuddle, germs, hug, deal with*). Student C will need to be encouraged *not* to read the texts (there won't be time) but to make notes along the lines indicated and find out everything during the interviews. Students A and B

should also be encouraged to make notes or underline points in the article. In the programme itself SS should use the facts but not read from the texts. Suggested organisation: e.g. in a class of twelve get the four 'A's, the four 'B's and the four 'C's to work together on the texts; then split up into four groups with one 'A', one 'B' and one 'C' in each group to prepare the programme.

If possible record the programme on audio/video tape. Possibly determine a particular style of programme (as in Unit 13), e.g. 'popular' or 'serious'.

## WRITING

### Linking words and expressions

Linkers have been practised in Review Unit 3 and Unit 8. The linkers practised here include many 'attitude' words (e.g. *unfortunately*) which help to make a text personal and natural. Encourage SS to use them in their own personal writing in English.

● **Exercise 1**   PW(?) or compare in pairs.

● **Exercise 2**   Another opportunity to practise advice expressions (see Units 9 and 15) if they have been introduced.

# Tapescripts

## RECORDING 1

sounds, go, way, fly

## RECORDING 2

'My friend's child is afraid of the phone ringing. If it rings loudly she puts a pillow over it and hides until it stops.'

# Key

## READING

### Reading

**1**

Touching things or being touched; leaves (especially rhubarb); agoraphobia; animals; objects; sex; being dirty; telephones; knives; swallowing food; cigarette smoke; white shirts; tunnels; bridges; spiders.

**2**

*Causes*: Largely a mystery. Possibly a depression or a shocking event.

*Symptoms*: Cold sweat, rapid pounding of the heart, rise in blood pressure, nausea, faintness, paralysing weakness of the limbs, going shaky, avoiding contact with what terrifies them.

*Treatment*: Facing the fear in a calm frame of mind, then forcing oneself to come into contact with what one is afraid of.

## VOCABULARY

### Adjectives into verbs

**1**

*Fear*: frightened, scared, terrified, petrified

*Symptoms*: feeling sick, going white, sweating, shaking, screaming, trembling, fainting

**2**

(See Exercise 1.)

**3**

frighten; scare; terrify (terrorise); petrify

## PRONUNCIATION

### Diphthongs

**2**

sounds /aʊ/; go /əʊ/; way /eɪ/; fly /aɪ/

**4**

sounds: *lou*dly

go: ph*o*ne, pill*ow*, *o*ver

way: afr*ai*d

fly: m*y*, h*i*des

## LANGUAGE POINT 1

### The *-ing* form

**1**

Travelling, moving, driving, doing, shopping, terrifying, boring, gripping, putting, eating.

**2**

shopping

## PRACTICE

**2**

b) the ordering

c) plenty of exercise is important for their health

d) preparing her lecture

e) telling me what to do

f) Sleeping in the park at night

g) the shopping

h) being quiet

## LANGUAGE POINT 2

### *-ing* or *to*?

**1**

*to* + base form: offer, deserve, refuse, learn, mean.

*-ing*: miss, feel like, deny, give up, put off.

**2**

a) to hit   b) eating   c) to escape   d) reading

e) laughing   f) to find

**3**

a), b), f)

## PRACTICE

**1**

Examples:

b) A: I *can't afford* to eat in restaurants.

   B: Don't worry. I've *decided* to cook you a really nice meal.

c) A: I really *dislike* travelling by train.

   B: In that case I'll *arrange* to go with someone else next time.

d) A: I really *enjoy* watching horror films.

   B: Do you *want* to watch this film on video?

e) A: You *promised* to buy me a portable phone for Christmas.

   B: I *can't stand* using those things!

**2**

a) to put   b) to help   c) running   d) to play

e) wondering   f) seeing   g) to understand

h) going

## WRITING

### Linking words and expressions

1 c)   2 a)   3 b)   4 b)   5 c)   6 a)   7 c)   8 a)

9 c)   10 b)

# Tales of the unexpected

## Students' Book

**General theme:** strange feelings.
**Unit topic:** psychic experiences.

**READING:** an article about a psychic experience.
**LANGUAGE POINT 1:** Past Perfect.
**LANGUAGE POINT 2:** Past Perfect or Past Simple?
**LANGUAGE POINT 3:** Past Perfect Continuous.

**VOCABULARY:** *make* or *do*?
**LISTENING:** a ghost story.

**SPEAKING:** story telling.
**READING AND WRITING:** comparing two different stories.

## Workbook

**READING:** extracts about people's psychic experiences.
**GRAMMAR:** Past Perfect or Past Simple?; Past Perfect Simple or Continuous: sequencing events.
**VOCABULARY:** ways of speaking (*whisper*, etc.); *say, speak, tell* or *talk*?; *make* or *do*?.
**PRONUNCIATION:** diphthongs (/eə/, /aɪ/, /aʊ/, /əʊ/).

## Language

This unit focuses on the Past Perfect and Past Perfect Continuous. The main use of the Past Perfect is to show that something in the past happened before another event in the past (e.g. *When I got up it had stopped snowing.*). This is contrasted with situations when two Past Simple forms are more appropriate, either because it is already clear from the situation (often by using time connectors) that one action happened before the other or because the two actions happened soon after each other – the second often as a result of the first (*When I saw him I ran up to him.*).

The Past Perfect Simple (for completed actions) is contrasted with the continuous form, which is used to describe actions in progress over a longer period of time up to or near the time in the past referred to (e.g. *Before I came to Britain I'd been working in Japan.*). If SS have grasped the nature of the continuous form (see Review Units 2 and 3 and Unit 13) and the Present Perfect, this should not be too much of a problem for them.

## Common problems
### Past Perfect Simple

**1** Some SS, e.g. Turkish speakers, over-use the Past Perfect and use it where they see events as separated from the present because they happened a long time ago (*\*I had visited my aunt ten years ago.*).

**2** SS often use the Past Perfect in situations where the Past Simple would be more appropriate (e.g. when the second action is a consequence of the first one): *\*When she had seen John she immediately turned away.*

**3** Practice is needed in both recognising and producing the contracted form – *I'd/he'd*, etc. SS often find it very difficult to hear the difference between, e.g. *I walked* and *I'd walked*.

**4** Mistakes are often made with Past Participle forms – Past Simple forms are often used instead (*\*I had went.*). Past participles need constant revision.

## Past Perfect Continuous

**1** SS often avoid the continuous form. Many languages have no continuous form and many SS find the aspectual problem (i.e. the focus on the action in progress) difficult to grasp.

**2** SS need to be reminded of verbs which do not take the continuous form (see Review Unit 2).

**3** SS sometimes find the form difficult to use spontaneously. They need practice in recognising and using both the contracted form (*He'd*) and the weak form of *been* in e.g. *He'd* (/hi:d/) *been* (/bɪn/) *waiting for ages when she finally arrived.*

# READING

● **Exercise 1** This is a prediction activity, to get SS' interest and give them a purpose for reading the text which follows. Use the photographs to introduce vocabulary which will come up in the text. PW/GW?

● **Exercise 2** SS should read the text once quickly for gist. (Alternatively, get SS to look at the questions in Exercise 3 first and guess what the story will be about.) Check to see if their guesses about the story were correct. Before reading the text intensively, possibly revise the linking words first by asking SS to group them under the functions they perform (i.e. *addition, time, contrast, result, reason*) and/or by getting SS to invent sentences to exemplify them. Refer SS back to Review Unit 3 and Unit 7.

# LANGUAGE POINT 1

## Past Perfect

If SS seem unsure about the use of the Past Perfect give them a few more examples, e.g. write a few past events on the board or use visuals to elicit a series of events from SS. Show how you can relate the events in sequence, using the Past Simple and time markers such as *and* and *then* (e.g. *Last Saturday I cleaned the car, went shopping, ironed a pile of clothes and cooked lunch. Then, at 12.30, my daughter finally got up.*) or how you can begin at the end and go back further into the past by

using the Past Perfect (e.g. *When my daughter finally got up, I was exhausted. I'd cleaned the car, ironed the clothes*, etc.). Tell SS that using this structure can help to make their story writing a little more varied.

# PRACTICE

● **Exercise 1** Remind SS about what a paragraph is, and its purpose. You may need to explain what Disneyworld is (i.e. a huge leisure complex), and that it is in Los Angeles. If necessary, give SS further practice in re-ordering a sequence of events using the Past Perfect.

# LANGUAGE POINT 2

## Past Perfect or Past Simple?

● **Exercise 2** An analytic activity. PW/GW? Focus on the fact that when the time sequence is ambiguous (i.e. when it is not clear from the time expression, e.g. *when*) whether one event happened before another, the choice of Past Simple or Past Perfect is important to the meaning of the sentence. If necessary, use timelines to make the use or 'concept' clear (see the *Language reference*).

Make it clear that with some time expressions, (e.g. *after, as soon as*) the sequence is usually clear enough to make the Past Perfect unnecessary, unless the speaker wishes to stress the fact that one event happened before the other.

# PRACTICE

Perhaps do these examples together as a class to make sure that SS have understood LANGUAGE POINT 2. There is more practice in the WB.

# LANGUAGE POINT 3

## Past Perfect Continuous

The 'concept' of an event in progress is often difficult for SS to grasp (although it has come up before in Review Units 2 and 3 and Unit 13). Possibly ask SS a couple more 'concept questions' to check they have understood it, e.g. which of the two verbs (*travel/spend*) focus more on activity in progress and which on the completed action. You may need to remind them of verbs which do not take the continuous form.

# PRACTICE

● **Exercise 1** PW/GW? Possibly 'get the ball rolling' by setting up the situation and getting SS to predict why Kevin and Susan had had such a good time before you get them to look at the pictures.

● **Exercises 2 and 3** These activities involve SS making a choice of which forms to use, and will show you if they have understood the 'concept'. PW/GW followed by class discussion? Encourage SS to discuss the reasons why they chose one form and not the other. If necessary, be prepared to go back and give further explanation/examples. There is more practice in the WB.

Exercise 3 is a 'freer' activity': encourage SS to be creative.

# VOCABULARY

## *Make* or *do*?

● **Exercises 1 and 2** *Make* and *do* is an area that SS have a lot of problems with. Tell them the general 'rule' but indicate there are many exceptions (as the dialogue shows), which they will have to learn as they go along. Encourage them to keep lists of *make* and *do* verbs in their vocabulary books.

● **Exercise 3** SS could act out this dialogue in pairs. Encourage them to use 'angry' intonation – possibly exaggerating an example as a model.

# LISTENING

● **Exercise 1** These words are connected to hospitals and operations. Allow SS to use dictionaries. Try to encourage them to make the link between the words and so guess where the story is set and what might happen.

● **Exercises 2–4** The listening is divided into three parts so that SS can predict what will happen at the end of each part. Try to encourage a build-up of tension and SS' guesses. It is quite a difficult recording, so SS will probably need to listen to it at least twice (possibly in a language laboratory). Alternatively, let them read the tapescript (full edition of the SB only) at the same time. Among difficult words you might want to pre-teach are: *lad, scruffy looking blighter, chuffed, het up, glower, stab, came to, lounging.*

Note that there is potential here for revision of indirect speech by reporting what the people in the story said.

# SPEAKING

● **Exercises 1–3** You may prefer to read the story extract aloud for maximum dramatic impact. Get SS to use their imaginations as much as possible and insist they do not just tell the basic information – the idea is that they embellish the story as much as possible, using adjectival and adverbial phrases.

● **Exercise 4** Having decided on the story-line, one of the group could record the story and then the rest of the group could listen and suggest improvements. Insist that they listen for accuracy of past forms, linkers, pronunciation, vocabulary, etc. as well as dramatic effect (adjectives, adverbs, intonation, etc.). Alternatively, at this point SS could record their own stories individually on audio or video tape and either monitor their own performance or ask other students to help them.

## READING AND WRITING

The aim of this activity is for SS to become more aware of what makes a good narrative. By this stage of the course, they have touched on most of the areas that combine to make a good story – narrative verb forms, adjective and adverb formation, linking expressions, punctuation, etc. Encourage discussion of the two different styles, and then get SS to write up the story in the SPEAKING section (or another story) using the list of features in Exercise 3 as a checklist.

# Tapescripts

### RECORDING 1

**Heart to Heart, by MD Stevenson**
'He seems to be doing well, doesn't he, Sister? He should be coming round pretty soon.'

I've got news for you, Nursie, he's come round already, even if he hasn't got his eyes open. I suppose I did have a vague impression of being wheeled out of the recovery room, but now – now I know I'm safely back in my special private ward. Yes, and with some other poor devil's heart beating inside me, doing very nicely too, thank you. Oh yes, the full treatment going now and two nurses on duty – one of them's a looker, anyway. There's a young lad over in the corner, too. I wonder what he's doing. Scruffy looking little blighter, even in a mask and white coat. Oh well, I suppose he's monitoring something or other. I can't really believe it yet. I made it! Mind you, the consultant always said I would. Nice old boy, Mr Walton.

'You're tough, Jim,' he told me. 'I wouldn't attempt this operation if you were one of these nervous imaginative types, but you'll come through it all right.'

By God, he was right. That young lad doesn't take his eyes off me. I made it.

### RECORDING 2

The consultant was chuffed when he saw me this afternoon. 'A wonderful job, Jim.'

I couldn't resist asking him, even though I knew I wouldn't get much of an answer. 'What was he like, this donor bloke? An accident, was it?'

Mr Walton put on that superior surgeon look that he doesn't wear very often. 'You could say that, I suppose. Don't you worry, Jim. You'll make better use of it than he would have done.'

Well, at least I know it was a man's heart.

The nurses are bustling about again. They don't take a lot of notice of that young lad – almost brush him aside, you could say. God I'm tired again.

Mr Walton was a bit less enthusiastic today. Something about not getting all het up. I'm not getting het up, dammit. I'm not awake long enough to get het up. I'm bored though. 'What about the telly?', I asked him. 'Or at least a look at a newspaper?'

'We'll see, Jim,' he promised. You see, nothing too good for the VIP patient. I forgot to tell him about the young lad, though. Pity. He's still over there, glowering. Miserable little devil.

### RECORDING 3

They're working like mad on me. All of them, and I can't do anything but lie here, helpless. I can't even tell them … I …

It was the paper that did it. Mr Walton brought it in himself.

'Here you are, Jim. Read all about yourself!'

It was there, too. On the front page. 'Mr James Wetherall was given the heart of a twenty-year-old youth, killed in an accident.' First time I'd ever managed to get my name in the papers. It was when I turned over the page I saw it.

*Killer Dies in Police Chase*
A youth of twenty died after the car he had stolen left the road during a police chase. Previously he had been involved in a fight in which a twenty-eight-year-old man was stabbed to death.

And that was as far as I got, because there was a picture, too. It was him – the lad in the white coat in the corner. Like the consultant said, I'm not an imaginative type, but I'd swear the picture is of that youth who's been there day and night, not taking his eyes off me.

I must have passed out when I realised it. And when I came to, there was this lot round me. And me, I can't move and I can't speak. I can only look, across to the corner where that youth is still lounging, looking back at me. And he's smiling now, damn him. He's smiling.

# Key

## READING

**2**
a) because  b) But  c) so  d) However
e) until  f) and  g) When  h) after that

**3**
a) To get some money in his will.
b) He had told them before he died.
c) He'd changed his mind.
d) To tell them he'd left them some money.
e) It had 'got lost in the post'.

## LANGUAGE POINT 1

### Past Perfect

**1**
Statement b) is correct.

## PRACTICE

**1**
Correct order: d), a), e), c), b)

**2**
a) ... they hadn't realised how huge Disneyland was.
b) ... he'd just given a good lecture.

## LANGUAGE POINT 2

### Past Perfect or Past Simple?

**1**
Giving a good lecture.

**2**
In the first sentence I went to bed *before* he arrived, and in the second sentence I went to bed *after* he arrived.

## PRACTICE

a) As soon as I saw him I fell in love with him.
b) Judy didn't want to read his latest novel until she'd read his others.
c) When they opened the drawer they found the money.
d) After she'd told him the news he left at once.

## LANGUAGE POINT 3

### Past Perfect Continuous

a) No.  b) Yes.

## PRACTICE

**1**
**2**  They had been sailing every morning.
**3**  They had been going to nice restaurants at lunchtimes.
**4**  They had been shopping in the local markets in the afternoons.
**5**  They had been out dancing nearly every evening.

**2**
a) left; had been snowing (*possibly* snowed)
b) didn't begin; had seen
c) didn't go out; had fed; (had) watered
d) left; had been working; (had) made
e) didn't know; arrived; had started
f) had been; got

## VOCABULARY

### *Make* or *do*?

**2**
a) doing; making
b) doing

**3**
1 make  2 do  3 do  4 did  5 made  6 do
7 (You)'ve been making  8 make  9 make
10 doing  11 doing  12 do  13 made  14 do

**4**
Flatmates. Tina seems to own the flat.

## LISTENING

**2**
a) His heartbeat being monitored.
b) In hospital.
c) He has had a heart transplant.
d) A young lad.
e) We don't know.
f) Not the imaginative type.

**3**
a) Who the donor of the heart was.
b) Because he wants to know who the donor was? Because of the young lad?
c) Watch the television or read a newspaper.
d) Because he has had a heart transplant.

**4**
a) He has passed out.
b) Who the donor was.
c) He saw the other article about the 20-year-old killer dying in a car accident.
d) Jim is going to die?

# So strong

## Language

This unit focuses on the passive. Some practice has already been given in Unit 10 on the Future Passive and SS have been exposed to passive forms in many of the texts. It is assumed that most SS can recognise the 'meaning' of a passive construction in context.

Some kind of passive construction exists in most languages but English uses passives more frequently than other languages.

### Common problems

**1** In many languages (e.g. French) active constructions are used with impersonal forms when in English the passive would be used (*On parle l'anglais. / English spoken here.*).

**2** There are many other subtle differences in form and use. For example, in Scandinavian languages the passive can also be expressed with the suffix -*s* (typical mistake: *\*It finds not.*). In Japanese, passives are mainly made about people and it is difficult to construct passive sentences for inanimate objects, like *The house was burgled.* In most languages except English the indirect object cannot be the subject of a passive verb in sentences like *He was given a watch for his birthday*, so this can cause problems.

**3** Many non-European SS have problems with the form of the passive (e.g. in the use of the verb *be* for both passive and active constructions: *was given / was giving*), and to many ears the whole construction can sound clumsy and formal. While it is true that the passive is used mainly in written texts such as notices, newspaper articles, etc., it can also be found in spoken English (*The train's been cancelled.*).

**4** One of the most frequent uses of the passive in English is to allow the speaker to position important pieces of new information at the end of an utterance in order to give it more stress ( see the *Language reference*, e.g '*Hamlet' is a marvellous play. It was written by* **Shakespeare**.). This use is often ignored in traditional grammar books and SS may well be unfamiliar with it.

Notice that exercises in the unit link the use of the passive to specific contexts and deal with its use as a way of focusing on events rather than who or what causes them. In English the form is used naturally and does not involve conscious change from active to passive forms.

Notice, too, that the *get* + past participle construction (often used instead of *be* + past participle: *He got run over* …) has been avoided in order not to confuse at this level.

## SPEAKING 1

The focus of the unit is on prejudice, in particular racial prejudice – a very sensitive subject which needs careful handling, particularly in classes of mixed race.

The police advertisement in Exercises 1 and 2 aims to get us to examine our own prejudices and stereotypes (the popular British assumption would probably be that the black man is a criminal rather than a policeman). If possible, show the SS the photograph without letting them see the caption. If not, get pairs/groups to work on the picture and caption together. The word *prejudice* is probably understandable (and therefore 'teachable') in context. Possibly, ask SS if there is racial prejudice – not necessarily against blacks – in their own country (in some classes it would be better to focus on Britain and the USA). Perhaps discuss the problems of housing, jobs and education for racial minorities (if possible, in a positive way). (This discussion could be saved to the end of the unit.)

● **Exercise 3**   Opens out the topic from racial prejudice to discrimination and prejudice against other groups of people. It links in with the theme of discrimination against women in work in the WB LISTENING.

## LANGUAGE POINT

### The passive

● **Exercise 1**   Ask SS to ask each other or check in their dictionaries for difficult words, e.g. *abusive, hooligans, taunted, menaced, blade* (or give near-synonyms for SS to match with these words). Check SS' understanding of the text (e.g. *'Was the man in the grey overcoat alone? Why was he attacked? Why is he still frightened?'* etc.). Possibly

draw attention to the dramatic-sounding journalese (a style focused on in Unit 13).

● **Exercise 2**   Beware complications in text, e.g. *by himself* in an active sentence – possible confusion with *by* as an agent in passive sentences; the *was* in the second paragraph connects with five past participles (*set upon, taunted, knocked, kicked, menaced*); *he is frightened* where *frightened* is used as an adjective. However, at this level, and because it's not SS's first exposure to the passive, it should cause no real problems.

Follow up Exercise 2 by writing one of the passive examples on the board (e.g. *He was set upon by a gang of hooligans.*) and comparing the structure with its active 'equivalent': *A gang of hooligans set upon the black man.* After doing Exercise 3, ask SS why the passive is preferred in the article (i.e. because names of the attackers are unknown and the event and the victim are more important).

## PRACTICE

● **Exercise 1**   Point out, for example: the formal 'distancing' tone of many passive sentences; that the passive is often but not always used in written contexts; that in headlines/notices the verb *be* is often omitted (e.g. *Man killed in racist attack*). Possibly give SS some other headlines to work out (e.g. *Shots fired at plane, Forest fires brought under control*).

● **Exercise 2**   Elicit other examples from the SS.

● **Exercise 3**   Make sure SS only use agent (*by*) if natural.

## VOCABULARY

### Collocation

The importance of this area is often underestimated. SS need a good dictionary which will give help both in the definitions and in the examples. (To illustrate, refer SS to the entry in the *Longman Dictionary of Contemporary English* for the word *draw*.) Get SS to practise linking consonants and vowels together (e.g. *drew a knife* /druːəˈnaɪf/). It is worth encouraging SS to have a section in their vocabulary books for e.g. *draw, have* and *get* and add other words that collocate as they come across them. Show how they can make it visual (e.g. as a 'network').

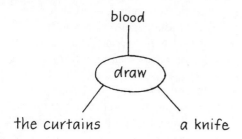

## PRONUNCIATION

### Contrastive stress

'Conversations are full of negotiation. Speakers often want to assert a fact or opinion quite strongly, deny what another speaker has said and offer correction, or ask about alternatives and options in order to come to an agreement about what to do. Learners of English need to be aware of this use of stress (i.e. contrastive stress) in order to follow discussions, arguments, and exchanges of opinions. The ability to use stress in this way is also a useful speaking skill.'
(from *Teaching English Pronunciation,* page 65 – see *Bibliography*)

Show SS that by giving prominence to certain words you are showing the relative importance of different parts of the message (possibly link the idea to language of telexes, notes and messages – see Unit 11). Show how flexible sentence stress is and that it is within the speaker's control as a tool to help him/her communicate.

● **Exercises 1–4**   Focus on recognition and purpose.

● **Exercise 3**   In dialogue a) notice that the word *dog* is stressed in *I like the dog.* because the speaker is introducing the topic into the conversation. Notice that there are several different ways of distributing stress in the dialogues (a–d), depending on the speaker's purpose. Possibly show SS how a sentence could be stressed in several different ways to give different meanings.

● **Exercise 5**   Gives practice – possibly extend into other exercises (see *Teaching English Pronunciation,* pages 65–69).

## LISTENING

● **Exercise 1**   Encourage SS to use their imagination. Perhaps ask them to jot down as they listen words they feel are important. Notice the structure: *The higher … / The taller …* etc.

● **Exercise 2**   Point out that words like *barriers* express an idea, not a thing (i.e. they are metaphorical); that *Brothers and Sisters* probably refers to fellow blacks. Try not to make comprehension work too heavy – some of the ideas/images might be difficult for SS.

 Possible follow-ups: ask SS if they know and could bring in any other songs about prejudice (racial or otherwise); bring in another one yourself (e.g. *Across the Lines* by Tracy Chapman).

## SPEAKING 2

This activity will not be suitable for every class (especially those that have not seen or do not relate to pop videos), so *optional.* Or simply get SS to discuss a few ideas about what a pop video could include.

 Possibly show examples of pop videos.

 You could encourage one group to be impressionistic, one to have a story-line, one to focus on the singer, etc.

## READING

● **Exercises 1 and 2**   Possibly (in some classes) elicit what SS know about South Africa (e.g. *'Who is the President? What is a 'township'? What changes have there been in recent years?'* etc.). Use questions a) and b) in Exercise 1 as prediction.

● **Exercise 3**   Get SS to read without dictionaries at this stage.

● **Exercise 6**   Could extend into: *'What do the following phrases tell us?'* e.g. *'I was working late at the Herald.'* (line 14); *'Whites only.'* (line 88). Other extension ideas: GW? What impression do we get of: a) Edward Simelane; b) van Rensberg; c) life in South Africa? (Give reasons.) Also, a discussion on racial prejudice (see notes for SPEAKING 1) e.g. *'Is it common in every country? Causes?'* etc. However, be careful: a powerful subject, needing tact, lots of ideas and good language skills (not for every class).

Notice use of narrative tenses and direct speech in the story. Both could be revised before the CREATIVE WRITING in the next section. Also, possibly, re-write parts of the direct speech in indirect speech.

# CREATIVE WRITING

Revise the punctuation of direct speech (see the WRITING exercise in Unit 16 in the WB).

● **Exercise 1** (GW/PW?) Brainstorm ideas.

● **Exercises 2 and 3** Possibly group stories or individual stories compared in groups. Perhaps best to focus on creativity rather than on grammatical accuracy.

# Tapescripts

## RECORDING 1
[See Key.]

## RECORDING 2
[See Key.]

## RECORDING 3
[First verse of (Something Inside) So Strong.]

## RECORDING 4
[The rest of (Something Inside) So Strong.]

# Key

## LANGUAGE POINT

### The passive

**1**
Walked, threatened, spoke, was (abusive), was (black), was set upon, taunted, knocked, kicked, lay, menaced, is (frightened), will happen, will not allow, to be published.

**2**
*Active*: walked, threatened, spoke, was (abusive, black), lay, will happen, will not allow
*Passive*: was set upon, taunted, knocked, kicked, menaced, to be published

**3**
Statement a).

## PRACTICE

**1**
a) 6   b) 4   c) 1   d) 3   e) 2   f) 5

a) Sounds formal and impersonal. It is the policy of the railway company.
b) The verb *be* is often omitted in headlines to make them shorter. Headlines tend to focus more on the event than the doer – here the doer is probably unknown. The passive is more often found in written than spoken English.
c) In many other languages, the active is used for notices; the English prefer the passive for impersonal expressions. Potential customers are not interested in 'who' speaks English in the shop.
d) The passive gives a sense of authority and distance. Note that the passive can be used in spoken English.
e) The passive is used to describe a process when we are less interested in – or don't know the identity of – the doer; the focus is on the process itself. The passive is therefore frequently found in scientific reports.
f) The focus is on the material, not who made it.

**2**
b) *White Christmas* was sung by Bing Crosby.
c) The *Mona Lisa* was painted by Leonardo da Vinci.
d) Australia was discovered by Captain Cook.
e) *Sherlock Holmes* was written by Arthur Conan Doyle.
f) The 1990 World Cup was won by West Germany.

**3**
a) Keith was nearly hit by a bus while he was trying to cross the road.
b) Luckily, not many people are struck by lightning.
c) Relations between the police and the community shouldn't be harmed by the incident.
d) All trains to Scotland have been cancelled because of the heavy snow.
e) She is being interviewed by the police officer.
f) My stereo and television have been stolen.

## VOCABULARY

### Collocation

*draw*: to a halt, the curtains, blood, a cheque
*have*: a bath, a look, a baby, a cold, a party, a rest, a
holiday, (a cheque)
*get*: ready, lost, a cold, angry, (a rest), (a holiday), (a
cheque)

## PRONUNCIATION

### Contrastive stress

**1**
PAT:   Where do you *live*?
JULIE:  On the second *floor*.
PAT:   I thought you lived on the *fifth* floor.
JULIE:  No, *Colin* lives on the fifth floor.
PAT:   Surely Colin has an *office* on the fifth floor but he
actually *lives* on the second floor?
JULIE:  No, Colin has *never* lived on the second floor. He
*lives* on the *fifth* floor and has an *office* on the
*ground* floor. *I* live on the second floor.

**2**
Julie stresses the words she regards as important often as a
contrast to disagree with something Pat says (e.g. *No,*
**Colin** *lives on the fifth floor.* – i.e. not *you*).

**3 and 4**
a)  A:  I like the *dog*.
    B:  *That* dog?
    A:  Yes, it seems a very *friendly* dog.
    B:  You're kidding. It's the most *vicious* dog I've ever
seen.
    A:  Well, *I* like it.

b)  A:  Why are you running so *fast*?
    B:  I'm not *running*. I'm *jogging*.
    A:  *Jogging*? You're *not*!
    B:  I *am*. I used to run *twice* as fast as this.

c)  A:  They serve *wonderful* fish there.
    B:  Yes, but the *meat's* disgusting.
    A:  You're *right*. And the *wine's* awful.

d)  Example:
    A:  English is a *really* difficult *language*.
    B:  Not as difficult as *French*.
    A:  Well, the *vocabulary's* more difficult.
    B:  Yes, but the *grammar's* hard in French.
    A:  And the *pronunciation* is awful in both.

## LISTENING

**2**
a)  The barriers to keep my race – the blacks – from sharing
in society as equals?
b)  The whites with power?
c)  The rights to equality, jobs, housing, education, etc.
d)  Powerful desire? will power? strength?
e)  You (the whites) won't be able to tell lies about me.
f)  'they' are the whites; 'we' are the blacks; 'good
enough' to live with them as equals.
g)  Get our rights? Become equal?

## READING

**1**
a)  Amazed? delighted? suspicious? proud? embarrassed?
b)  *Whites*: angry? insulted? pleased?
    *Blacks*: proud? suspicious? contemptuous?

**2**
c), b), a), d)

**4**
a)  look sideways …
b)  quiet thoughts about
c)  began to move
d)  unnaturally limited …
e)  took the conversation …
f)  forced out
g)  if I am not

**5**
a)  hardly anyone
b)  confidentially
c)  encounter
d)  abreast
e)  unwillingly

**6**
a)  A (Although embarrassed, he is secretly proud.)
b)  A (He doesn't take himself too seriously.)
c)  B, C (van Rensberg is unusually casual and friendly in
his attitude to Simelane – which tells us that such a
thing between white and black was a rarity in South
Africa.)
d)  B (C) (He is sensitive to the hard life of blacks.)
e)  B, C (Again, he shows sensitivity to the prejudice
against blacks. We see the social gap between the
races.)
f)  C (Rigid rules inhibit the freedom of blacks.)
g)  A (Simelane has a curious nature.)
h)  B, C (van Rensberg's friendliness would normally cause
a stir.)
i)  A, C (Simelane is too shy/suspicious, possibly of building
a bridge of friendship with someone from the other
race – the atmosphere of the country is against it.)
j)  A, C (He is in white territory and this is 'apartheid'.)

## CREATIVE WRITING

The story actually continues with Simelane having an
uneasy drink of brandy with van Rensberg in the passage
outside his flat. He is not invited in. Van Rensberg had
hoped that the barriers between black and white could
have been broken down, but the problem cannot be
solved that easily. Van Rensberg drives Simelane back to
the station. When Simelane gets back to Orlando, he tells
his wife the story and she weeps.

# Revision

## Students' Book

**LISTENING:** a traditional aboriginal story, *Wilar the Crocodile*.
**READING:** vocabulary, and a story called *The Great Whale's Mistake*.
**GRAMMAR AND FUNCTIONS:** present and past forms; the future; making dialogues; conditionals and *wish*; spot the errors.
**VOCABULARY:** guessing vocabulary in context.
**PRONUNCIATION:** sentence stress.
**WRITING:** description.

## Workbook

**GRAMMAR:** review of verb forms; sentence transformation; spot the errors.
**VOCABULARY:** word building; test your vocabulary.
**PRONUNCIATION:** sounds – vowels and diphthongs.
**WRITING:** linking expressions; dictation.

## Organisation and aims

This unit is divided into two main parts: a 'skills' section and a language revision section.

The first part includes a listening text and a reading text, which are both stories and require additional work on vocabulary (including the use of dictionaries), and guided summary writing. The second part of the unit contains language exercises covering many of the areas studied in this book. There are exercises on all the main tenses, and conditionals, and some work on language 'functions' such as 'offering', 'giving and asking for permission', etc.

This unit could be handled in one of several ways. The listening and the reading texts are probably best done in different lessons and possibly combined with some of the revision exercises in the second part of the unit. In any case the language work is probably best split up so that some is done in different sessions. The language exercises could be done by SS either individually, as a test, or in pairs. However they are done, feedback on SS' performance and follow-up remedial work will be important.

Another way of exploiting this unit is to treat it as a 'resource bank' to pick and choose from – the listening and reading could be done at any time towards the end of the course, as could many of the language points. However, *Present and past* and *Spot the errors* are probably better left until the end, as they include examples of the Past Perfect and passive forms not covered until Units 18 and 19.

## LISTENING

Before the SS listen to the story, explain that 'the Dreamtime' was a time when the aboriginal people of Australia believed that the land and the animals were created. Explain also that there is a strong story-telling tradition in Australia based on these creation myths, of which *Wilar the Crocodile* is one. The stories are not just myths or folk stories but have immense cultural importance for the Aborigines – not only because of their religious significance but also because they put the people in touch with the land and environment in which they lived, and are still relevant to their traditional life today (see *The Songlines* by Bruce Chatwin). The land is identified as God, and the animals are also worshipped and respected for their cunning and potency. The frogs in the story, for example, are seen as fruits of the land and the water.

Get SS to try and predict from the illustrations what the story might be about, and introduce the main characters (Wilar the Crocodile and the two sisters, Indra and Jippi) before they listen.

● **Exercise 1** SS listen for gist.

● **Exercise 2** PW? SS try to answer the questions and then listen again more carefully to check their answers. An opportunity to revise the form and pronunciation of regular and irregular Past Simple verbs and also linking expressions.

● **Exercise 3** This is a writing activity, with focus on verb forms and linkers. It is important that SS completely understand the story before they attempt the summary. This summary could either be done individually, as a test, or in pairs. SS could also record their stories on tape before or instead of writing it up. In the feedback, go back to Review Unit 3 and Unit 8, if necessary, and do remedial work on linkers.

As a follow-up SS could exchange creation myths and legends from their own cultures, orally and/or in writing, or invent one themselves. For some story-telling ideas see *Once Upon a Time* (see *Bibliography*).

# READING

● **Exercise 2** Dictionary work, including looking up definitions and revising the phonemic script. Make it clear that *adolescent* can be both a noun and an adjective.

● **Exercise 3** An oral fluency activity used as a prediction exercise. Encourage SS to use their imaginations and guess what the story might be about. Ask them what they think the 'Great Whale's Mistake' might be.

● **Exercises 6 and 7** Exercise 6 involves reading for specific information and Exercise 7 requires SS to 'read between the lines' and make deductions. You could perhaps ask SS if they have any similar stories to tell.

Follow-up work could be along the lines of SS 're-writing' or inventing a traditional story (e.g. *Red Riding Hood*) seen from a different perspective (e.g. through the eyes of the wolf).

# GRAMMAR AND FUNCTIONS

## Present and past

You might want first to ask SS one or two questions to check comprehension of the text. The gap-fill could be done individually or as PW, and could be followed by a discussion on which verb forms SS chose and why. Use the opportunity to do remedial work on problematic areas.

Perhaps allow SS to use dictionaries for the vocabulary in this text. Difficult vocabulary to highlight: *on the right tracks, probation scheme, go straight, let down.*

## Future

Could be followed by a discussion of the answers. If any remedial work is necessary there are exercises in the WB.

## Making dialogues

Probably best done in pairs. This activity includes some functional language covered in the book. Possibly do revision of the language and the intonation. This exercise could be done at any time after Unit 14.

## Conditionals; *wish*

This exercise could be done at any time after the completion of Unit 12.

## Spot the errors

PW? This could also be done as a kind of 'Grammar auction' class activity, where SS 'bid' for the sentences which they think are correct (see *Grammar Games* – details in the *Bibliography*).

## VOCABULARY

### Guessing vocabulary in context

This section tests SS' ability to deduce the meanings of words from the context, and also tests their awareness of word formation (prefixes, suffixes, etc.).

## WRITING

### Description

The notes for the letter could be prepared in groups, with SS brainstorming ideas. These ideas could then be elicited and perhaps put up on the board under paragraph headings. An opportunity here to do revision of descriptions (see Unit 7). Make it clear to SS that you will be looking for accurate use of present, past and future forms. Tell them to monitor their work carefully for these things before giving their work in.

The letter could be written at home or done in class as a writing test. Alternatively, SS could write the letter as groupwork.

# Tapescripts

### RECORDING 1

This is a story about Wilar the crocodile. One day, a long time ago when the world was very young, there were two sisters. One was called Indra and her younger sister, Jippi. They had been walking for a long time and they sat down to have a rest near a river. Wilar, the crocodile man, was in the river and he saw them. And he said to himself, 'I'm going to have one of those girls.' He swam through the river, and the girls didn't see him coming. And when he got close enough, he grabbed Indra. Jippi was very frightened and ran away screaming for help.

Wilar took Indra back to his cave. He didn't want to eat her yet, so he left her in the cave and he went back to the water where he caught himself lots of fish to fill up his belly.

When he came back to the cave, Indra was asleep: she was very tired and frightened. Wilar didn't want to touch her yet, so first he put a lot of mud and stones in the entrance to the cave so that other crocodiles couldn't come in and disturb him. Then he said to Indra, 'You are my wife now, and I am going to stay with you.'

Wilar didn't leave the cave for several days, but then when his belly was empty and he got hungry again, he had to go out and look for food. Before he left the cave he blocked it up again with mud and stones to keep the girl safe, but also to stop her running away.

When Indra found herself alone, she decided she'd try and break through the entrance, but the stones in the entrance were so heavy and it was hard to shift them. She couldn't do it with her hands, so she tied her hair around the stones and began to pull the stones away from the mud.

When she'd made a hole in the entrance she tried to squeeze her way through. She got her head and her chest through, but her belly was so big, she couldn't get out. She had to come back inside the cave and make the hole bigger. Finally she managed to push her way out and run away.

Of course many people were looking for Indra and with them was her sister Jippi. Jippi saw Indra running from the cave and she shouted to the others. She said, 'Look, my sister is coming back.' When Indra reached them, Jippi noticed she had such a big belly. She said, 'Sister, why are you so fat? You must have eaten a lot of fish.' But Indra didn't answer her. Instead she squatted down near the ground and out of her belly came a big pile of crocodile eggs.

Well, the men hit the eggs with their clubs, and every time they broke an egg a frog came out and jumped away. Some of the frogs went to the water, and some of the frogs went to the country. That was the first time frogs came into the world, and they can live in both places because their father came from the water and their mother came from the land. The frog doesn't have any hair because Indra lost all her hair when she pulled the stones away from the entrance to the cave.

### RECORDING 2

[See Key.]

# Key

## LISTENING

**1**

1 B  2 C  3 E  4 D  5 A

**2**

a) Incorrect. Wilar had decided he would have either one of the girls.
b) Incorrect. Jippi ran away screaming.
c) Correct.
d) Correct.
e) Partly correct. But he also wanted to stop other crocodiles getting in.
f) Incorrect. He went away to find food.
g) Correct.
h) Incorrect. She was pregnant.

**3**

a) While Indra was having a rest near the river Wilar grabbed her.
b) He took Indra to his cave. However, he did not want to eat her yet so he went to catch some fish.
c) Although Indra was frightened she was also very tired and she fell asleep.
d) Wilar put mud and stones at the entrance of the cave so that other crocodiles could not come in.
e) He told Indra she was his wife and he was going to stay with her.
f) As soon as Indra was alone she tried to escape.
g) The stones were heavy so she used her hair to move them.
h) After she had made the hole big enough she escaped and ran away.
i) When Jippi noticed her sister's big belly she thought Indra had been eating a lot of fish.
j) The men hit the crocodile eggs that Indra produced.
k) Some of the frogs which jumped out of the eggs went to water and some went to the country, because their parents had come from both places.

## READING

**4**

Possible answer:
This story looks at human beings and their destruction of the world from the point of view of the whale.

**5**

a) ton  b) sludge  c) dump  d) spout

**6**

a) Because 'school' is a collective noun meaning a 'group of whales'.
b) Because they just lie on the beach staring at the ocean and when they go in the water they get in the way of the whales.
c) To keep down the hot dog population, or to make rubbish.
d) The equivalent of their 'God'?
e) They must live peacefully with it.
f) A car or a van.

**7**

a) The creation of people.
b) He talks about pollution (sludge, oil) which is spoiling the whale's habitat.
d) Examples of humour:
  – The writer reverses the role of whales and humans: e.g. the whales talk about a 'school of humans'; 'the Great Whale' is equivalent to our God-figures; the whales regard humans as inferior life forms.
  – The writer presents an outsider's view of the strange things that people do: e.g. lying on sand and boiling themselves in oil (for sunbathing).
  – The writer refers to things the whales don't understand in a humorous way: e.g. 'metal boxes' for cars, 'hot dogs' as real animals ('the hot dog population').

## GRAMMAR AND FUNCTIONS

### Present and past

1 paid
2 wasn't invited / hadn't been invited
3 were sleeping
4 broke in
5 had been burgled
6 received
7 had been caught
8 his prison address was
9 felt
10 have been
11 was allowed
12 had been sent
13 is trying
14 has become
15 calls
16 plays
17 has even gone / has even been / has even been going
18 used to spend / spent
19 was all stolen
20 have made

### Future

a) 're leaving; 'm going to live
b) going to be mended
c) are you going to buy; 'll look
d) 'll have
e) 'm meeting

### Making dialogues

Examples:
a) A: Good morning. Can I help you?
   B: Yes. This necklace that I bought here last week has broken already, so would you mind refunding my money, please?
   A: I'm afraid I can't. The necklace was in a sale, and we don't give refunds for sale items.
   B: Well, I'm not prepared to accept that. I'd like to see the manager, please.
b) A: Could I use my dictionary, please? I need to look up a word.
   B: No. I'm sorry, but you aren't allowed to use dictionaries during the exam.
   A: Well, could I go to the toilet then?
   B: Of course you can. You don't need to ask.

c)  A: Excuse me. Could I have a word? Would you mind getting the manager?
    B: Certainly, madam. Could I ask what it's about?
    A: Yes, this fish isn't fresh.
    B: I'm terribly sorry but there were no fish deliveries this morning. Can I get you a steak, instead?
d)  A: When do I have to pay the rent?
    B: You must pay me weekly and in cash.
    A: Can I keep a dog?
    B: Sorry, pets are not allowed.

## Conditionals; *wish*

a)  were; 'd get
b)  had
c)  would you; were/lived
d)  'd; had
e)  went; 'd be there
f)  were; would spend
g)  were

## Spot the errors

a)  'How much *does the computer cost*?' 'I'm sorry, I don't know how much *it costs*.'
b)  In 1907 *Norway* became *the* first country to give *the* vote to *women*.
c)  I enjoyed the cake *(which/that)* we've just eaten.
d)  The shops close early today, *don't they*?
e)  I must *hurry*! I want *to get* there on time.
f)  Unfortunately, the company now has *few* clients.
g)  Beverly *told* me she was very unhappy.
h)  Jamie *hasn't been* to work *for* two days now.
i)  This week's much colder *than* last week.
j)  There's not *much* rice left. Go and get me *some*, please.
k)  'I can't remember the address.' 'No, *neither can I*.'
l)  Julia suggested *leaving* before it got dark.
m) I told her I wasn't hungry as I *had* already *eaten* lunch.
n)  We were *invited* to the party by the Managing Director.
o)  Has Patricia *been told* that her sister is ill? If not, please tell her as soon as possible.

# VOCABULARY

## Guessing vocabulary in context

b)  fliglive = *thirsty* (adjective)
c)  tralets = *examinations* (noun)
d)  trodly = *badly* (adverb)
e)  sarked = *arrived* (verb – past tense)

# PRONUNCIATION

## Sentence stress

A:  I don't really like the *smell*.
B:  Well, *I* don't really like the *taste*.
A:  *Don't* you? Why *not*?
B:  I think it's *awful*.
A:  It cost a *fortune*. We *ought* to *eat* it.

# Language index (Students' Book)

# Language index (Workbook)

# Bibliography

Some of the following books are referred to in the Teacher's Book.
All have been an invaluable source of information and ideas to us
and we recommend them to teachers for their own reference.

ALEXANDER, L.G. *Longman English Grammar*
(Longman, 1988)

BAKER, A. *Ship or Sheep*? (Cambridge University
Press, 1977)

DAVIS, P. and RINVOLUCRI, M. *Dictation*
(Cambridge University Press, 1988)

ELLIS, G. and SINCLAIR, B. *Learning to Learn
English* (Cambridge University Press, 1989)

FRANK, C. and RINVOLUCRI, M. *Grammar in
Action* (Pergamon, 1983)

GAIRNS, R. and REDMAN, S. *Working with Words*
(Cambridge University Press, 1986)

GRELLET, F. *Developing Reading Skills*
(Cambridge University Press, 1981)

HEDGE, T. Writing (Oxford University Press, 1988)

KENWORTHY, J. *Teaching English Pronunciation*
(Longman, 1987)

KLIPPEL, F. *Keep Talking* (Cambridge University
Press, 1984)

LEECH, G. *An A–Z of English Grammar & Usage*
(Edward Arnold, 1989)

LEWIS, M. *The English Verb* (Language Teaching
Publications, 1986)

*Longman Active Study Dictionary of English*
(Longman, 1983)

Longman Dictionary of Contemporary English
(Longman, New edition – 1987)

McALPIN, J. *Longman Dictionary Skills Handbook*
(Longman, 1988)

MORGAN, J. and RINVOLUCRI, M. *Once Upon a
Time* (Cambridge University Press, 1983)

MORGAN, J and RINVOLUCRI, M. *Vocabulary*
(Oxford University Press, 1986)

MORGAN, J. and RINVOLUCRI, M. *The Q Book*
(Longman, 1988)

O'CONNOR, J.D. *Better English Pronunciation*
(Cambridge University Press, 1967)

O'CONNOR, J.D. and FLETCHER, C. *Sounds
English* (Longman, 1989)

RINVOLUCRI, M. *Grammar Games* (Cambridge
University Press, 1984)

ROGERSON, P. and GILBERT, J.B. *Speaking
Clearly* (Cambridge University Press, 1990)

SWAN, M. *Practical English Usage* (Oxford
University Press, 1980)

SWAN, M. and SMITH, B. *Learner English*
(Cambridge University Press, 1987)

UR, P. *Discussions that Work* (Cambridge
University Press, 1981)

UR, P. *Grammar Practice Activities* (Cambridge
University Press, 1988)